Joyful Recovery From Chronic Fatigue Syndrome/ME

Strategic Book Publishing
New York, NewYork

Joyful Recovery From Chronic Fatigue Syndrome/ME

Accelerated Healing With Emotional Freedom Techniques (EFT)

Sasha Allenby

BA Hons, PGCE, EFT AAMET Trainer, Adv PSYCH-K®,
Dip. Shiatsu, Cert. Yoga Teaching, Dip. LC, Dip. NLP

JOYFUL RECOVERY FROM CHRONIC FATIGUE SYNDROME/
ME: ACCELERATED HEALING WITH EMOTIONAL FREEDOM
TECHNIQUES (EFT)

Book and cover design: G. Holmes

Printed in the United States of America

ISBN 978-1-60693-145-5
SKU 1-60693-145-8

Published by Strategic Book Publishing
An imprint of AEG Publishing Group
845 Third Avenue, 6th Floor - 6016
New York, NY 10022
www.StrategicBookPublishing.com

Disclaimer
While EFT has produced remarkable clinical results, it must still be
considered to be in the experimental stage and thus practitioners and
the public must take complete responsibility for their use of it. Further,
Sasha Allenby is not a licensed health professional and offers EFT as
a personal performance coach and holistic therapist. This book is not
intended to diagnose your condition, or to substitute medical advice.
Please consult qualified health practitioners regarding your use of EFT
and the techniques presented in this book.

Dedication

This book is dedicated to three remarkable people: my partner Rupert Wood, who lovingly supported me through my recovery from ME; EFT Master Karl Dawson, whose teachings guided me on my journey to health; and Gary Craig, founder of EFT, whose contribution to the healing movement will be remembered for an eternity.

Contents

• If EFT doesn't work for you

Other Things You Can Do To Support Your Healing

- Accept the illness

- Use positive language

- Live in "soft time"

- Take a naturopathic perspective on healing

- Release your anger about the injustice surrounding ME

- Surround yourself with positive, healthy people

- Learn about and apply the "Law of Attraction"

- Learn to climb your emotional scale

- Journal your progress

- Have a "Glad of the Day"

- Make a "Well Done Me!" list

- Balance your life

- Have some fun

- Adopt a spiritual perspective

- Learn present-moment awareness

- Invest in the *Holosync* program

- Invest in biofeedback software for your computer

- Learn deep relaxation

- Affirm your health

- Visualize your health

- Get the right nutrition and supplementation

- Consider exercise

- Get your energy flowing

- Find a Perrin practitioner

- Find a PSYCH-K® practitioner

- Educate yourself

- Research, but don't search

- Stop watching the clock!

- Avoid watching or reading things that depress you

- Take the "21-Day Complaint-Free Challenge"

- Make a contribution to others

- Love yourself and others!

- Relax and discover the joy of living!

Foreword

Using Emotional Freedom Techniques to overcome CFS/ME is a subject very close to my own heart. Six or seven years ago, I had become increasingly ill with chronic fatigue, multiple allergies, inflammation, metabolism and blood sugar regulation issues. EFT formed a very substantial part of my healing journey.

Whilst recovering from these autoimmune conditions and becoming an EFT therapist, trainer and eventually EFT Master, I seem to have drawn a disproportionate amount of clients and trainees who were themselves overcoming ME, CFS and other immune-related health problems.

The universe has a way of sending not only those who are on a similar path but also, if we pay attention, the solutions to our problems. So while I looked for the answers to help myself and my clients heal, I was lucky enough to find wonderful teachers from around the world.

Gary Craig, the creator of EFT, was one such teacher. Donna Gates, the founder of the Body Ecology Diet, and cellular biologist Dr Bruce Lipton were other pioneering and inspiring teachers, whose incredible knowledge helped me make sense and understand the conditions I and others were experiencing. Health conditions for which the modern medical model had no solution.

Armed with a wealth of information from these great people, I developed the *EFT for Serious Disease* training, which has been popular with therapists and lay people alike. It explains how eventually, as we age, our core beliefs and early childhood experiences, if left unresolved, often manifest as a myriad of diseases as the body tries to adapt the subconscious mind's mistaken perceptions of self and the environment. EFT can support a journey back to health and help maintain that healthy state. I have seen impressive results, not just with ME and CFS but also with conditions such as rheumatoid arthritis, MS, IBS, diabetes, asthma, cancer, Crohn's disease, colitis, vitiligo, alopecia, hypothyroidism, anxiety, panic attacks, stress and depression, amongst many other physical and emotional conditions.

Over recent years I have been blessed to support many ME clients and trainees on their journey to health. One such exceptional trainee was Sasha. When she originally came to my training she was in the early stages of her recovery from ME, and was still extremely weak. It has been a great pleasure not only to help her return to health, but to see her develop as a truly gifted practitioner and trainer, and see her practice flourish and grow to be an excellent success.

I am very pleased that Sasha has written this book. It is a wealth of resources. It will be a great companion to lay people who are overcoming ME, and an excellent guide for EFT practitioners and other health professionals. It combines a balance of the cutting-edge developments in bodymind science, with easy-to-follow instructions on EFT. It also provides the reader with an overview of how to use EFT to overcome ME, and other practical and solution-focused approaches to moving through the condition.

So whether you are overcoming CFS/ME, an experienced EFT practitioner, or a newcomer to EFT, there is plenty in this book for you. Use it wisely, at a pace that suits you, and whatever comes up… *keep tapping with EFT!*

Love and hugs,
Karl Dawson
EFT Master
Karl is one of only 29 EFT Masters worldwide. Visit his website at http://www.efttrainingcourses.net.

Introduction

About this book

T his book is an introduction to how Emotional Freedom Techniques (EFT) can support and maximize your recovery from Chronic Fatigue Syndrome (CFS), Chronic Fatigue Immune Deficiency Syndrome (CFIDS), Myalgic Encephalomyelitis (ME), Post-Viral Syndrome, (PVS) or Fibromyalgia (FM). You will learn about the incredible benefits of EFT, and how it can help you to overcome your condition by healing your body and mind simultaneously.

You will be introduced to the growing field of scientific evidence which supports the understanding that the mind and body are one. This book also outlines that to heal from any health condition, we have to concentrate not only on healing the physical being, but on healing the whole person.

What you will get from this book

This book has been created to help you see recovering from CFS, CFIDS, ME, PVS or FM in a whole new light. It will enable you to take your healing into your own hands, presenting you with practical techniques that will support your physical and emotional recovery.

It will help you to begin to identify any limiting beliefs that you have about healing that may be holding you back, and give you suggestions on how to move through them.

At the end of the book there are other practical suggestions that will help you heal your condition, alongside using EFT. There is also an extensive reading and resources section at the back of the book, to further your knowledge and understanding.

If you are a health professional, an EFT practitioner, or a practitioner of other healing modalities, this book will help you to gain an overview of how you can best help your clients who are overcoming CFS/ME.

For doctors and other medical professionals, this book will support you in a greater understanding of your CFS/ME patients.

Who I am

I have written this book from my own personal experience of overcoming a severely disabling case of ME using Emotional Freedom Techniques. I have over a decade's experience in holistic therapies, including EFT, PSYCH-K®, shiatsu, life coaching, yoga teaching, pilates and personal training. I also have a background in teaching and lecturing.

In the past I have worked using drama as a therapy with disturbed and disaffected children and adolescents, and trained senior management in schools on how to deal with problem behaviors effectively.

I now work as a full-time Advanced Practitioner and Trainer of EFT, and also as an Advanced PSYCH-K® Facilitator. I have a national and international client base and a busy workshop and training schedule. I specialize in overcoming CFS/ME, with an emphasis on helping my clients and workshop participants to return to the joy that is their birthright.

Evidence of EFT to support recovery from CFS/ME

There are many success stories from those who have used EFT to support their journey to health from a variety of conditions. These include a whole host of health challenges including CFS, lupus, multiple sclerosis, diabetes and cancer. These success stories can be found on the popular worldwide EFT website, http://www.emofree.com.

Stories specific to CFS/ME are also currently being compiled, and can be accessed at http://www.eft-me.co.uk.

How to use this book

If you are reading this as someone who is overcoming CFS/ME, then this book is designed to help you help yourself. My suggestion is that you read it all the way through first, and highlight sections, thoughts or ideas that may apply to you. When you have a complete overview of the techniques and tools presented in this book, you could then return to the relevant sections, and work on what is appropriate to you.

Important note regarding the science presented in this book

It is important to note that although there is a selection of scientific research presented in this book, you do not need to understand the science behind bodymind for EFT to work effectively. It has been included for those who prefer a scientific perspective, but you can access all the techniques in this book without a grasp of the science presented here.

Chapter 1

ME/CFS: A PHYSIOLOGICAL CONDITION

Before continuing any further, it is vital for the reader to understand that I fully recognize ME or CFS as a physiological, organic condition. As ME has a history of being wrongly labeled as a psychological condition, it is important that the reader fully distinguishes between the old misconception that ME is all in the mind, and the understanding being expressed in this book that all health conditions are in both body and mind simultaneously. What happens in our physiology also affects our psychology, and vice versa. This has been understood for thousands of years in the East, but has only recently become more widely understood in the West. We now have the scientific evidence to verify this ancient understanding, and this will be supported later in this book.

There is also much debate in the ME community about whether CFS and ME are separate conditions. This is not a debate that I wish to enter into in this book, so I am going to refer to CFS, CFIDS, ME and PVS simply as "ME" from here on, as EFT and the techniques presented in this book will benefit all these conditions, whatever their etiology or symptoms.

Evidence that ME is an organic condition

There is a wealth of research from a variety of sources to confirm that ME should be considered a physiological condition. Listed here are key samples from that research.

Dr Myhill's research on mitochondrial malfunction

Dr Sarah Myhill's research highlights how ME can result from a range of causative factors including infection, toxic damage, overwhelming stress, or vaccination. According to Dr Myhill, this leads to poor antioxidant status and mitochondrial malfunction of the cells. As the mitochondria help to generate energy, their reduced function leads to poor stamina and fatigue.[1]

The HPA axis

Other evidence is seen in the malfunction of the hypothalamic–pituitary–adrenal axis, or HPA axis, in those with ME. The hypothalamus is known as the master controller within your body. It regulates many systems and functions of your body through your glands, your vagus nerve, and via messenger molecules known as neuropeptides.

The hypothalamus regulates your immune system, which is your first line of defense. It controls your sympathetic nervous system, which produces emotional change. It affects the action of your heart, muscles, skin, and gut through your adrenal glands. It also directly controls your sleep function, your internal temperature, your appetite, your sex drive, your physical growth, and your tissue renewal.

In health, the hypothalamus maintains balance in the body, but in those with ME it becomes overactive and is unable to carry out this balancing act. According to Dr Raymond Perrin, a leading osteopath in the field of ME, this leads to an overload in the sympathetic nervous system. Dr Perrin highlights how this reduces blood flow and lymphatic drainage, leading to toxic build-up in the central nervous system.[2]

Essential fatty acid deficiency

Further evidence of physiological disruption in ME patients is found in the research of Professor Basant Puri, who is both a clinical consultant at London's Hammersmith Hospital and a senior research scientist at Imperial College, London.

His research indicates a number of key findings for those overcoming ME, which relate to the metabolism of fatty acids. One finding is around the chemical choline, which in health has a gradient in the brain, with more being found in the front of the brain and less in the back. Professor Puri found that in ME patients, this gradient does not exist and that the concentration of choline in the back of the brain is as high as in the front. He believes that the increased choline levels are related to abnormal metabolism in membrane phospholipids, the building blocks of all cell membranes in the brain. His study indicates that there is increased loss of fatty acids in the brain of those with ME, which can be addressed with the supplementation of specific essential fatty acids.[3]

Slow-wave sleep patterns

ME has also been associated with altered amounts of slow-wave sleep. In your waking state, your brain mainly generates *alpha* and *beta* waves. *Beta* waves occur during day time wakefulness, and *alpha* waves occur whilst you are awake but relaxing. During sleep, your brain switches to *theta* and *delta* waves. The slower the brain wave activity, the deeper the sleep. During a normal sleeping pattern, a person goes through four stages of sleep. Stages one and two are when you drift off and go into a slightly deeper sleep. Stages three and four are the much deeper stages, also known as "non-REM sleep" and "restorative sleep." In the deeper stages, the body heals and restores itself, but for those with ME there has been shown to be a deficiency of restorative sleep.[4]

Enterovirus in stomach

A study by John and Andrew Chia also found that CFS is associated with chronic enterovirus infection of the stomach. Their study points to CFS having a number of potentially treatable infectious etiologies, with enteroviruses being the causative agents in more than half of the 200 subjects that they tested.[5]

Altered gene signature

Research by Dr Gow reveals that there is a different gene signature in those with ME. Dr Gow found a particular pattern of genetic activity among those with ME, which contrasted to the gene signature of those who did not have the condition.[6]

Genetic subtypes of ME

Genetic research by Jonathan Kerr has also identified a biological basis for seven different subtypes of ME, all identified by a specific genetic pattern.[7]

ME as a body and mind condition

So ME is clearly a physiological condition affecting the neurological, lymphatic, immune, and endocrine systems, impacting almost every function in the body. Sadly, the misapprehension by certain members of the medical community that ME is a psychological disorder has created a taboo around the mental and emotional disruption that accompanies the condition. This is not helped by the fact that in Western medicine an illness is usually defined as either physiological or psychological. In other words, Western medicine often takes a very either/or approach to the mind and body, as if they were separate. In contrast, Eastern thinking looks at healing the whole person in *any* disease or condition, and it is this approach that we will be exploring further in this book. It may help to put aside any attachment that you might have to ME being either a physiological or psychological condition, and to read with an open mind to the information that follows.

Chapter 2

MY HEALING STORY

In the beginning

Like most who have experienced ME, I have a story of misdiagnosis, misunderstanding from doctors, severe physical pain, and emotional turmoil. But this book is not about reflecting on the negative, but rather focusing and building on the positive; so I will start my healing story from my turning point. This point came about 9 months into what was probably my second major experience of ME. At the time, I was totally disabled with the condition. I lay in bed for 20 hours a day, and rose only to eat and use the bathroom. I was severely depressed, because I could barely move, I had to be carried in and out of the bath, and I couldn't even put my own socks on. Nine months earlier I had been a very active and successful performing arts lecturer, holistic therapist, yoga teacher and life coach, and I was completely devastated by my loss of position and status.

Turning point

However, on the day of my turning point I came to realize that I was causing my own suffering. This does not mean I was to blame in any way for my situation or how I felt about it; it simply means that the thoughts I was choosing about my situation were adding to my misery. I realized that although pain was inevitable given my physiological condition, suffering was a choice. In that moment I made a decision to stop fighting my condition. I realized that continually telling myself over and over again that everything was awful, and that my life was over, was not going to contribute to my healing. I made a pledge to accept where I was and learn from it. I stopped labeling myself as someone who was suffering from ME, and started to refer to myself as someone who was recovering from ME.

When the student is ready, the teacher appears

What followed was a journey that was so profound that I am actually grateful to ME for what it has taught me about myself and the personal growth that has resulted from my transformation. Everything that I needed to learn in order to recover fell into my path and I was blessed with the right teachers, the right information, and the answers that I needed. Would these things have fallen into my path anyway without a change of thinking? I doubt that very much, as I believe that the enormous shift in my consciousness attracted the right circumstances for my healing.

Perrin Technique™

On a physiological level, I dealt with my condition using the Perrin Technique™ – a unique lymphatic drainage system for those who are overcoming ME. I was blessed to meet and work with Shirley Kay, an outstanding osteopath, naturopath and Perrin practitioner, who supported my healing on many levels. Shirley also introduced me to Metabolic Typing – a dietary system that assesses the macronutrient needs of each individual according to their body type – and I began to experience more energy. I made fantastic progress under Shirley on a physiological level.

The anxious perfectionist!

Psychologically, however, I still had many issues. Like most people who are challenged with ME, I was still very driven and highly anxious. I was a perfectionist, and my need to have everything in a certain order, and my misery and disappointment if this was not fulfilled, drove me to constant exhaustion. Also, for most of my life I had been plagued with invasive memories from my past and I still played them over in my mind constantly, as a matter of course. I searched for a resolution to this, trying various talk therapies with some positive results. But it wasn't until EFT came into my life that I had a massive shift on this front.

My first encounter with EFT

Originally, I discovered EFT as a form of pain relief for ME. My first experience of it was phenomenal. I had crippling and constant pains in my calves, which felt like battery acid dripping through my nervous system. I had been awarded Disabled Living Allowance due to these pains, which had been present for around 15 months when I discovered EFT. I learned the EFT sequence from a book and applied it to myself as an experiment. After 5 minutes, I experienced a sensation like ice cracking up the back of my legs. I felt a shooting pain go from my legs, up my back, and seemingly out of the top of my head. At the same time, I uncharacteristically burst into tears. I cried for several minutes and then stopped cold. The pain in my legs that had crippled me so badly was completely gone.

EFT practitioner training

Following this phenomenal first experience, I went on an Emotional Freedom Techniques practitioner training with EFT Master Karl Dawson, who himself overcame chronic fatigue-related health issues by using EFT. At the start of the first 3-day training that I went on, I would say I was 40% recovered from ME. By the end of the 3 days, I was 70% recovered. So to what did I owe this miraculous turn-around? It was not just because I dealt with my physiological symptoms using EFT. In fact, the physiological symptoms were only the tip of the iceberg. It was most definitely because I had spent 3 days dealing with the trauma from my childhood and life in general, that contributed to my wrong beliefs and thinking about myself and the world. This was at the root of the physical illness that I was experiencing, and in the rest of this book I will explain how the psychology affects the physiology in this way.

A multidisciplinary approach

It is important to note that I am not claiming that EFT alone healed my condition. I took a multidisciplinary approach to my healing, which included dietary changes and supplementation. I worked, as mentioned earlier, with a Perrin practitioner. I practiced yogic breathing and full relaxation at least twice a day. I changed my diet and took supplements. And I also shifted the remainder of my condition with another technique known as PSYCH-K®. But by far the biggest impact on my health was identifying the trauma that came from my upbringing and life experiences, and changing it with EFT.

Finding your own path

If in this moment you find yourself thinking that you do not have the courage or the strength to change in this way, then please do not despair. The techniques presented later in this book are designed to help you shift your thinking about your condition, and clear the root emotional issues that are preventing your physiological healing.

Are you feeling skeptical?

I feel it necessary to also include a note to any skeptics here, who may doubt that I had ME in the first place. A number of times I have read of people who have recovered from ME using the Lightening Process, or other alternative modalities, only to have members of the ME community decide that the person in question can't have had ME, if it was so easily cured. So, for any among you who are doubting that I had the condition, I was diagnosed on four separate occasions in the UK: firstly by a specialist in CFS/ME at the Stroud Hospital; also at Bristol Frenchay Hospital for CFS/ME; further by my doctor; and finally by Raymond Perrin, leading osteopath in the field of ME.

I had every single biological marker for the condition, which had started with a virus from which I didn't initially recover. My symptoms included severe fatigue and muscle pain that worsened on exercise, and severe and debilitating mental and physical fatigue. I had influenza-like malaise, frequent sore throats, and enlarged glands. I experienced depression, brain-fog, poor memory, poor concentration, and constant headaches. My sleep was non-refreshing and disrupted. I had environmental and chemical sensitivities, over 20 food allergies, and digestive problems. My body temperature fluctuated constantly, and I had noise and light sensitivity. I was also tested at an independent laboratory and found to have essential fatty acid deficiency. And I am now 100% healed from ME, with absolutely no symptoms whatsoever.

Chapter 3

AN INTRODUCTION TO BODYMIND

The body as machine

In the West, there has been a tendency since the emergence of Newtonian physics to see the body almost as a machine. Western medicine has tended to view illness as a kind of mechanical breakdown that needs to be fixed with chemical or surgical intervention. However, in recent decades there has been a greater recognition of the link between health and emotions among Western doctors. But a duality still appears to exist in many people's understanding of the connection between mind and body. On the one hand, we know that the mind affects the body. If we think a stressful thought, we release adrenaline and our heart rate increases. If we remember a time we were embarrassed, our face reddens. And we have begun to name stress as one of the biggest killers of the modern age. However, our understanding of the bodymind connection is often quite simplistic, and we generally overlook how our thoughts, beliefs and emotions can trigger disease.

Psychoneuroimmunology (PNI)

Despite our lack of thorough understanding, the fascinating scientific field of psychoneuroimmunology, or PNI, is deepening our understanding of the connection between mind and body. This specialist field of research studies the relationship between psychological processes and the immune and nervous systems of the body, and how they communicate with each other using various chemical messengers. This field has helped us enter into a new understanding of human psychology and physiology and the links between stress and disease.

In her book *Everything You Need To Know To Feel Good,* world-renowned psychopharmacologist Dr Candace Pert points out that:

> [C]ontrary to the reigning paradigm belief, the body doesn't exist merely to carry the head around! [...] Instead, the brain itself is one of many nodal, or entry points into a dynamic network of communication that unites all systems – nervous, endocrine, immune, respiratory, and more.[8]

And we shall see from the following examples that the mind can work with the endocrine and immune systems, or against them, creating sickness or health.

Examples of the mind working against the body

There are many thousands of examples of the mind working against the body. In his powerful book *Healing Breakthroughs: How your Attitudes and Beliefs Can Affect your Health*, Dr Larry Dossey, himself a practicing clinician, describes a case where a patient who was allergic to penicillin was given a placebo drug – an inert substance with no known biological effect. After the patient swallowed the placebo, he was told an "untruth": that the pill was not in fact a placebo, but penicillin. The man panicked, went into anaphylactic shock, and died immediately. His death was created by the meaning that he gave to the pill and his belief in the effect that would it would have on him.[9]

A further story in the same book highlights the plight of a middle-aged woman who had a narrowing of the tricuspid valve on the right side of her heart. She had experienced low-grade, chronic congestive heart failure, but medical intervention had allowed her to maintain her job and continue with household chores. On one occasion a noted heart specialist was taking a group of trainees on an examination tour. He entered the room, greeting the patient, and announced to the trainees that "This woman has TS," before leaving abruptly.

After the doctor left, the woman's demeanor changed suddenly, and she began to hyperventilate. She became drenched with perspiration and her pulse went up to 150 beats per minute. Her lungs, which had been clear minutes earlier, began to fill with fluid. When asked what was wrong she replied that the doctor had said that she had TS, which she believed meant "terminal situation." The doctor present explained that TS meant "tricuspid stenosis," which was the condition of her heart valve. She could not be reassured, her lungs continued to fill with fluid, and she lost consciousness. She died later that day from intractable heart failure.[10]

In the same book, Dr Dossey describes Black Monday Syndrome, and the astonishing fact that more fatal heart attacks occur on Monday at 9am than at any other time of the week. According to Dr Dossey:

[T]he best predictor for a first heart attack is not any of the major risk factors (high blood pressure, high cholesterol, smoking, and diabetes mellitus), but rather job dissatisfaction.[11]

It would seem that it is our thoughts and feelings about the loathing, dread or challenge of our work that create the heart attack.

In Dr Dossey's book, there are a whole host of excellent examples of how we can create sickness with the power of our thoughts.

Examples of the mind working with the body

However, with the same mind that creates disease or illness, we can also create amazing health. In his excellent book *It's The Thought That Counts: The Astonishing Evidence For the Power of Mind Over Matter*, pharmaceutical scientist Dr David Hamilton explores the nature of the placebo effect. Dr Hamilton became fascinated by the bodymind connection whilst working as a research scientist in the pharmaceutical industry. He repeatedly saw patients receiving placebo pills and reporting the same level of improvements as those receiving the actual drugs. Despite this, the placebo effect is brushed over in medical science, and even seen as an inconvenience to medical research. His fascination with the placebo effect caused Dr Hamilton to leave his position in the pharmaceutical industry and explore scientists, mystics and healers in the field of "bodymind" medicine.

Dr Hamilton reveals how research on the placebo effect highlights that most scientists agree that it works because of three main factors:

(1) A person's desire to be healed.

(2) Their expectancy that they are going to be healed, or that something positive is going to happen.

(3) Their belief that they will be healed, either because they believe in the medicine, or because they believe in the competency
of the medical staff looking after them.[12]

Dr Hamilton also adds a fourth factor: feelings, which are produced by the expectancy or belief in a person's ability to heal. He outlines that in numerous experiments it has been shown that:

[T]he degree to which you believe governs the rate at which
you are healed.[13]

Dr Hamilton cites various studies on the placebo effect. In one
study, a group of patients with Parkinson's disease, who usually received a drug injection for their symptoms, were instead given a harm-
less salt-water injection. Believing that they had received the usual
drug injection, they experienced relaxation of the muscles and could
move more easily. Remarkably, on monitoring the electrical signals to
their brain, real changes were shown in the areas of the brain that are
usually hyperactive in Parkinson's patients.[14]

Dr Hamilton also highlights a study carried out on pregnant wom-
en who were told that the drug they were given would stop their nausea
and vomiting. The women were also asked to swallow a device that
measured the stomach contractions associated with the nausea, so that
the experiment could be measured precisely. When they were given
the drug, the nausea and contractions stopped, as suggested. This was
confirmed by the measuring instrument that they had swallowed. However, the women were actually given a drug that should have made
them even sicker: syrup of ipecac. It seems that it was the power of
suggestion, coupled with their strong desire to feel better, that not only

resolved the symptoms, but was also able to override the substance that should have made them worse.[15]

A further study highlighted by Dr Hamilton was one in which a group of medical students were asked to take either a pink or blue capsule, and were told that the capsules were either a stimulant or a sedative. However, both capsules were completely inert. Interestingly, the blue capsules had more of a sedative effect than the pink ones, presumably because blue is the color associated with calm.[16]

Placebo versus nocebo effect in clinical practice

So from theses examples we can see that the mind can work to disrupt or heal the body. The body can create health with the placebo effect, or negate health with the nocebo effect. It is said by leading cell biologist Dr Bruce Lipton, in his book *The Biology of Belief,* that:

> Troublesome nocebo cases suggest that physicians, parents and teachers can remove hope by programming you to believe you are powerless.[17]

At the same time, Dr Lipton points out that there has also been a great undermining of the placebo effect by the medical community:

> [T]he "all in their minds" placebo effect has been linked by traditional medicine to, at worst, quacks, or, at best, weak, suggestible patients.[18]

This has been highlighted as a significant error by Dr Lipton, who believes that the placebo effect is glossed over in medical schools, not just due to dogmatic thinking, but also due to financial considerations (much of medical research being funded by the pharmaceutical industry).[19]

In the next three chapters, we will explore further the work of Dr Bruce Lipton, along with other key scientists who have made major contributions to the growing field of bodymind medicine. Through this exploration we will investigate the science behind how the mind affects the body in this way.

Chapter 4

DR BRUCE LIPTON AND
THE BIOLOGY OF BELIEF

The "New Biology"

One of the major contributors to the field of bodymind science is Dr Bruce Lipton, an internationally renowned cell biologist, author and former Stanford University lecturer. In his best-seller, *The Biology of Belief,* Dr Lipton shows how the cells of our body are affected by our thoughts, and how environmental signals control the activity of our genes. He is part of a growing field of scientists who are working with a new understanding of the human body, which has been termed the "New Biology." This New Biology recognizes the wisdom of the cells, and the effect that their environment has on them.

According to Dr Lipton, this new view of science will change civilization on a profound level:

This New Biology takes us from the belief that we are victims of our genes, that we are biochemical machines, that life is out of our control, into another reality, a reality where our thoughts, beliefs and mind control our genes, our behavior and the life we experience.[20]

Dr Lipton highlights that we no longer need to take a defeatist attitude and surrender to the mercy of our genes:

[T]he New Biology ... leaves in the dust the defeatism of genetic and parental programming as well as survival-of-the-fittest Darwinism.[21]

Our current popular scientific model of reality leans heavily on Darwin's theory of evolution. However, Dr Lipton outlines not only that this is a major error, but also that it was recognized as such by Darwin himself, who admitted later in his life that he had underestimated the role of the environment:

In my opinion, the greatest error which I have committed has been not allowing sufficient weight to the direct action of the environments, i.e. food, climate, etc., independently of natural selection... When I wrote the Origin, and for some time afterwards, I could find little evidence of the direct action of the environment; and now there is a large body of evidence.[22]

So Darwin recognized the flaw in his own theories – the very theories upon which our current model of medicine is built.

Dr Lipton highlights the problem with our belief that we are at the mercy of our genes, and our fear that we are subservient to their power. He points out that we live in a world filled with people who feel they are like ticking time-bombs, living in constant fear that their genes are going to turn on them.[23]

It is important to note, however, that Dr Lipton is not discounting the role of genes altogether:

Of course, there is no doubt that some diseases, like Huntington's chorea, beta thalassemia and cystic fibrosis, can be blamed entirely on one faulty gene.[24]

However, he emphasizes that the majority of us come into life without the impediment of faulty genes:

[S]ingle-gene disorders affect less than two percent of the population; the vast majority of people come into this world with genes that should enable them to live a happy, healthy life.[25]

He goes on to emphasize that in most diseases, the genes are not the main problem:

The diseases that are today's scourges – diabetes, heart disease and cancer – short-circuit a happy and healthy life. These diseases, however, are not the result of a single gene, but of complex interactions among multiple genes and environmental factors.[26]

For the vast majority of us, then, it would seem that there is not one single gene at error:

Scientists have linked lots of genes to lots of different traits, but scientists have rarely found that one gene causes a trait or disease.[27]

Environmental signals

The new field of science that explores how environmental signals control the activity of genes is known as "epigenetics." According to Dr Lipton:

For ninety-five percent of the population, if they are failing in health it is not something wrong with the genes and the proteins, it is something wrong with the body's signals. Inappropriate signals are the source of most human illnesses and dysfunctions.[28]

The three things that interfere with signals in the body are: trauma, when an accident causes a disruption in the brain signal; toxins, which interfere with the body's signaling chemistry; and the mind. If the mind sends inappropriate signals at the wrong times, our systems become imbalanced and diseased.[29]

So why would the mind send wrong signals to our body? Well,

according to Dr Lipton it is a matter of perception. Each cell has many thousands of protein receptors. The receptors enable the cell to read its environment. The receptors are like switches, and they respond to a massive amount of environmental signals. They control the function of our lives through awareness of the environment, and adjust our biology accordingly. If our perceptions are accurate, then this provides a positive means of survival. However, if we are programmed with misperceptions and inaccurately read our environment, we inappropriately engage our responses.[30]

Vital to our understanding of how genes work is the fact that perception also controls the read-out of the genes. How we see life ultimately determines which genes will be activated to provide for our survival. We can inappropriately activate our genes by sending the wrong signal at the wrong time, and thus cause disease and dysfunction.[31]

So, in Dr Lipton's words:

[P]erception "controls" biology, but [...] these perceptions can be true or false. Therefore, we would be more accurate to refer to these controlling perceptions as beliefs. Beliefs control biology.[32]

Programming and the subconscious mind

Of course, all this is not taking place consciously, but rather in the subconscious mind. Neuroscientists have revealed that 95–99% of our behavior is controlled by the subconscious mind. That means that the conscious mind is responsible for only 1–5% of our behavior, whilst the subconscious mind is responsible for more than 95% of our behavior.[33] The subconscious mind processes 20 million environmental stimuli per second, whilst the conscious mind interprets 40 environmental stimuli in the same second.[34] The conscious mind can handle just a few tasks at a time, while the subconscious mind can handle thousands of tasks simultaneously. Dr Lipton outlines that:

> The subconscious mind, one of the most powerful informa-tion processors we know, specifically observes both the sur-rounding world and the body's internal awareness, reads the environmental cues and immediately engages previously ac-quired (learned) behaviors – all without the help, supervision or even awareness of the conscious mind.[35]

Dr Lipton describes the subconscious mind as our "autopilot" and our conscious mind as our "manual control."[36] You may think with your conscious mind, but it is your subconscious that is in charge. Run-ning negative subconscious beliefs is therefore highly destructive for us as human beings.

But where do these negative subconscious beliefs come from? Well, according to Dr Lipton the answer is that they come from our life experiences, but particularly from our conditioning in the first 6 years of our lives. Between the ages of birth and 2 years old, babies are mostly in a state of *delta* brain wave activity, and between the ages of 2 and 6 children are predominantly in a state of *theta* brain wave activ-ity. *Delta* and *theta* are the brain-wave states that hypnotherapists drop their clients into in order to make them more suggestible. This explains why children are like sponges, absorbing the beliefs, attitudes, and be-haviors of the adults around them. And when we become adults, we keep the same programs that we received in childhood, unless we work to change our conditioning.[37]

**How do we change the programs
of the subconscious mind?**

For years the merits of positive thinking have been touted by various self-help gurus. Although positive thinking is an important part of your healing, and will change the way you feel on many levels, some people find positive thinking very challenging. This is because positive thinking takes place in the conscious mind, and does not affect the habits or behaviors of the subconscious mind.[38]

So how do we change the patterns of the subconscious mind and influence our destructive behaviors and patterns? Well, an understanding of the fact that we are all energy may be a good starting point. Quantum physicists have revealed to us that beneath our apparent physical structure there is nothing more than energy; we are, in fact, not solid matter, as previously thought, but beings of pure energy.[39] And our new understanding of this has created new and powerful approaches to help us influence our biology. Dr Lipton emphasizes that:

Conventional methods for suppressing destructive behaviors include drugs and talk therapy. Newer approaches promise to change our programming, recognizing that there is no use "reasoning" with the subconscious tape player. These methods capitalize on the findings of quantum physics that connect energy and thought. In fact, these modalities that reprogram previously learned behaviors can be collectively referred to as energy psychology, a burgeoning field based on the New Biology.[40]

Later in this book you will learn to apply Emotional Freedom Techniques, perhaps the most popular form of energy psychology, so you can influence and change the subconscious beliefs that are in turn affecting your biology.

Chapter 5

BRUCE LIPTON'S RESEARCH ON GROWTH AND PROTECTION

D r Lipton has also carried out fascinating research on our survival mechanism, and this research may be highly relevant to those overcoming ME. In *The Biology of Belief,* he highlights how our survival can be divided into two functional categories: growth and protection. Our growth does not stop when we reach adulthood, as every day billions of our cells wear out and need to be replaced. So on a cellular level, we continually need new growth in order to survive.

Also vital to our survival are our protective mechanisms, which help us to ward off threats from pathogens, and also to identify and respond to threats to our personal safety. Interestingly, Dr Lipton reveals how the mechanisms that support growth and protection cannot operate optimally at the same time. The human body is designed so that growth systems shut down when there is a perceived danger. This is so that we can put all our energies into escaping or overcoming the threat. For example, if you are digesting your food and you encounter a fierce dog, the priority for your body will not be to complete digestion but to go into fight-or-flight so that you can protect yourself. The stress signal triggers an adrenalin response, and blood will move out of your digestive system and into your arms and legs, enabling you to run and save your life. So protection is vital for our human function.

The body is protected by two main systems: the immune system, which protects you against internal pathogens, and the HPA axis, the system that protects you against external threats. You may recall that this is the same axis which is said to be overactive in those with ME.

Dr Lipton's research on the HPA axis

Without any external threats, the HPA axis is inactive and growth within the body flourishes. However, as soon as the hypothalamus perceives a threat from an environmental signal, this triggers the HPA axis into a fight-or-flight response. With the blood out of the visceral organs, your body can no longer do its life-sustaining work, and Dr Lipton explains that:

> ...the stress response inhibits growth processes and further compromises the body's survival by interfering with the generation of vital energy reserves.[41]

Once the HPA axis is triggered, the immune system is then repressed, so as to conserve your body's energy.

A further consequence of triggering the HPA axis is that our ability to think clearly is diminished. Dr Lipton highlights how:

Adrenal stress hormones constrict the blood vessels in the forebrain, reducing its ability to function.[42]

Therefore, although the HPA axis is an excellent mechanism for handling acute stresses, it was not designed to be continuously activated. But our current lifestyles, and the beliefs that we are running, put us in a hyper-vigilant state where we are constantly primed for action.

An excellent analogy of this continuous stress and sustained adrenaline response is described by Bruce Lipton in *The Biology of Belief.* Imagine a group of healthy sprinters at the start line of a race. At the command "On your mark," they take to their starting blocks. When they hear "Get set," they tighten their muscles and go onto their fingers and toes for action, awaiting the go command. The strain of the "Get set" mode only lasts a few seconds in a normal race, and in this time their bodies release adrenaline to power their muscles for the race ahead. However, in this mythical race, the "Go" command never comes, so no matter how fit the athletes are, they collapse from the strain of maintaining constant readiness on the starting blocks. Dr Lipton highlights how:

We live in a "Get set" world and an increasing body of research suggests that our hyper-vigilant lifestyle is severely impacting the health of our bodies. Our daily stressors are constantly activating the HPA axis, priming our bodies for action.[43]

Dr Lipton links this chronic state of stress to "almost every major illness that people acquire."[44]

Dr Lipton's research in relation to ME

Take a moment now to consider this research, and the implications it could have for those overcoming ME. First and foremost, if you are in a constant state of triggering the HPA axis, then this is suppressing your immunity. This could explain why you were not able to overcome the original virus that may have preceded your condition.

Next let us think about the assertion that belief creates biology, and consider how this relates to your condition. Remember, the HPA axis is triggered when it perceives a threat, but this perception is based on your upbringing and your life experiences. In fact, many of the perceived threats are not actually threats to our safety at all; we have just been programmed to respond in a certain way based on what has gone before. And this is the point where EFT comes in, because it can help you change your relationship to the stressors, so that your subconscious no longer perceives them as threats. This can change the response of the HPA axis. This is why Dr Lipton highly recommends EFT and is quoted as saying:

> EFT is a simple, powerful process that can profoundly influence gene activity, health and behavior.[45]

Later in this book, you will learn how to apply EFT to overcome any perceived threats that may contributing to your condition.

Chapter 6

CANDACE PERT AND
MOLECULES OF EMOTION

Emotional receptors

Another key contributor to the field of bodymind science is internationally acclaimed psychopharmacologist Dr Candace Pert, who has made a life-long study of the chemical links between our physical cell structures and our emotional experiences. What she discovered, along with her partner Michael Ruff, is that there are receptors for emotions on every cell of the body, and not just in the brain, as previously thought.

Prior to Dr Pert's research it was believed that when our emotions made us blush or feel bliss, for example, that the body was responding to a signal from the brain. Dr Pert's research reveals that these responses are actually being produced not just in the brain, but also in cells throughout the whole body.

Her research shows that the key to our emotional responses is found in tiny messenger molecules known as neuropeptides. In *Everything You Need to Know to Feel Good*, Dr Pert provides an elegant scientific explanation of how we experience our emotions on a cellular level. This explanation is paraphrased below, but can be found in greater detail in her book.[46]

Dr Pert outlines that every cell in the body has thousands of tiny receptor molecules on its surface, much like sense organs. Their role is to pick up signals from the space that surrounds them. When a signal is received by the receptors, it is transferred to deep within the cell. This directs the cell to divide and grow, spend or conserve energy, repair, or fight infection, and so on.

The signals communicate cell to cell through hormones, neurotransmitters and peptides, which are collectively known as ligands. According to Dr Pert, this provides "an infrastructure for the conversation going on throughout the bodymind."[47] These ligands are responsible for 98% of the data transferred in the brain and body. In particular, the peptides, of which there are over 200 in the brain and body, sound an "emotional chord – such as bliss, hunger, anger, relaxation, or satiety – when their signal is received by the cell." Dr Pert collectively calls the receptors and the ligands "molecules of emotion."[48] An example is the peptide, endorphin. When it binds to a receptor molecule on the surface of the cell, it triggers a feeling of well-being.

Dr Pert explains that it used to be thought that the ligands find the receptors by a lock-and-key model, where the peptide or key would float by until finding its perfect key receptor or key hole, and this unlocking process would allow cellular activity to begin. However, it is now understood that this is only partially accurate. Dr Pert outlines how the more dynamic relationship between receptor and ligand involves vibrational attraction. The receptor actually resonates, "creating a vibration that resonates with a ligand vibrating at the same frequency, and they begin to resonate together."[49]

Therefore, Dr Pert refers to peptides and receptors as "the molecules of emotion" because:

> [T]he emotions are the link between the physical body and nonphysical states of consciousness, and the receptors on every cell are where this happens. The attracting vibration is the emotion and the actual connection – peptide to receptor – is the manifestation of the feeling in the physical world.[50]

So we can now see that our cells are intelligent entities. The mood-altering neuropeptides are active not only in our brains, as traditionally thought, but also in our blood, muscles, bones and organs.

So what does all this mean for us in terms of our emotional experiences? The answer, according to Dr Pert, is that within our bodies the receptors modulate our physiology in response to our experiences. She highlights how "Emotions influence the molecules, which in turn affect how we feel."[51]

Importantly, the peptides do not latch on to one single receptor, as previously thought. The receptors are actually clumped tightly together, and they form "multiple complexes." Dr Pert reveals how these clumps of receptors create deep channels leading to the interior of the cell, and establish a pumping action as they open and close. She highlights that:

> As they move these channels let substances in and out of the cell, setting up an ionic flux, or electrical current which can course through the bodymind.[52]

Importantly, Dr Pert also explains how this current influences the way that we think. This is because one of the things it does is "influence the firing 'set-point' in the brain, determining the path of brain-cell activation."[53]

However, Dr Pert emphasizes, this does not mean that the peptides and receptors produce the emotion in a cause-and-effect relationship. Instead, she explains that the molecules are actually the emotions, and not their cause. She says that the feelings we have are, in actuality, the "vibrational dance that goes on when peptides bind to their receptors." Beneath our feelings, a phenomenal amount of emotional information is being exchanged on a subconscious level. This has led Dr Pert to assert that "Your body is your subconscious mind."[54] Her research helps us to understand on a scientific level that the mind and body are not separate, as previously thought, but are in fact one.

The work of immunologist Michael Ruff

Further connection between health and the emotions can be found in the work of Dr Pert's husband, immunologist Michael Ruff. In *Everything You Need To Know To Feel Good*, Dr Ruff presents a lecture which highlights that disease is not simply a result of microorganisms such as viruses or bacteria:

[T]here are two components to disease: the agent that causes it, [...] and the way the body reacts to that agent.[55]

He explains that our emotions are an important part of the equation in health:

[A] person's emotional state plays a major role in how well

he or she is able to fight off infections.[56]

Dr Ruff asserts that with our new perception of bodymind, we can now understand how emotions and information can create an environment in which systems are closed down, and healthy functions are interfered with, which impedes wellness and sustains the disease process. He says:

[M]emory [...] is stored or encoded in cells at the level of the receptor throughout the bodymind. When we experience a traumatic event, physical or psychological, an emotional component of that trauma exists in the body as well as the brain. For the most effective healing, then, it makes sense to engage the entire bodymind, not just the brain or body.[57]

He also explains that in order to heal the past, it is helpful to gain some awareness of stored trauma:

[I]f you are not aware of memories and traumas stored in your bodymind, you can't do anything about them. So the first step in healing or recovery must involve awareness of where your past and injuries are stored, and then making an attempt to unravel them.[58]

So how do we unravel these stored memories and past injuries, and interact with our emotions to help them flow freely? Well, this is where EFT comes in. EFT is highly recommended by Dr Candace Pert, who is quoted as saying that "EFT is at the forefront of the new healing movement."[59]

EFT can help you effectively remove the effects of trauma from the mind and body, and support a healthy flow of emotions.

Chapter 7

INTRODUCING EMOTIONAL FREEDOM TECHNIQUES (EFT)

Gary Craig's worldwide phenomenon

EFT is a form of energy medicine, or, more precisely, a form of energy psychology. It was founded by Gary Craig, an incredible individual who has single-handedly made it a worldwide phenomenon. It has been labeled "the most talked-about therapy of the new millennium," and many leading health professionals in the field of bodymind medicine are suggesting that it may be the most important new therapy in modern medicine. It is used widely by internationally recognized medical doctors such as Deepak Chopra, Norm Shealy, and Eric Robbins. It has also been popularized by the likes of Paul McKenna and Dr Joseph Mercola. It is starting to become more commonly used in organizations such as the UK National Health Service, in schools, and in therapeutic clinics worldwide. Although often combined with other practices, it is highly effective as a stand-alone therapy. Its popularity has risen due to the fact that it has swift and lasting effects, and often works where nothing else will.

Originally adapted from Roger Callahan's Thought Field Therapy, EFT is a much more simplified and accessible version of its predecessor. It is based on the Traditional Chinese Medicine meridian system – the same system that has been used for thousands of years in acupuncture. In fact, EFT is often described as a form of emotional acupuncture, but the important distinction is that in EFT no needles are used. Instead, a series of points on the body's meridian system are tapped with the fingers. Whilst the points are being tapped, the recipient brings to mind and verbalizes, in a very specific manner, a health issue or emotional problem that they are experiencing. This causes changes in the body's energy system, and helps to release stored emotions or patterns of illness from the body.

More about your body's energy systems

To understand how EFT works, we must make the distinction between the Western interpretation of energy in the body, which is derived from food, sleep, sunlight, air, etc., and the Eastern concept of subtle energy, which is the life-force that flows within us. It is this life-force that EFT is working with. When we are in good emotional and physical health, this life-force flows through various energy systems in our body. One of these energy systems is the meridian system – a series of energetic pathways that run through our body, which cross over and connect with each other at various points. Each meridian has acupoints on the skin which, if stimulated through pressure or tapping, move energy through the meridian system.

Many ancient Eastern practices such as tai chi, qi gong, acupuncture, acupressure and shiatsu were designed to keep the meridian energy flowing to support health and well-being. However, trauma and stress in its many forms create blocks in this energy system, which leads to illness and disease. In fact the founding statement of EFT, made by its originator Gary Craig, is that "the cause of all negative emotion is a disruption in the body's energy system." EFT works to release this disruption so that energy can flow freely.

Your body and your emotions

In her book, *Everything You Need to Know to Feel Good*, Dr Pert highlights the importance of the emotions, which have often been overlooked in the traditional medical model:

> [T]he key that explains how energy heals, how mind becomes matter, and how we can create our own reality is the emotions.[60]

So why are the emotions so important? Let's consider, on a very basic level, what happens in your body when you have an emotional response. Most of your emotional responses take place on a subconscious level. They tend to come from either re-living traumatic memories from the past, or anxiety about what is going to happen in the future. When you remember something traumatic that has occurred or reflect on something that you fear might happen, your body chemistry changes. This is the mind affecting the body. It is not the memory of the past event or the thought of the future event that actually causes the problem. As discussed earlier, it is the meaning we attach to our thoughts that in turn alters our body chemistry. In fact, our subconscious mind cannot tell the difference between whether the event is happening now, in current time, or whether it happened in the past. Once the emotional response is triggered, our bodies go into fight-or-flight as if the memory or thought was really happening in current time.

Emotion memory

When I studied and lectured in performing arts, one of my favorite subjects was the work of Russian actor, director and producer Stanislavski, who is often referred to as the father of modern acting theory. One of his key techniques was "emotion memory." An actor would be required to think of a time that they were in similar situation to that of their character, and to evoke the emotions they had felt at the time, in order to portray the role convincingly. Every actor who has ever experienced recalling their emotions in this way will know that they evoke past emotions from every part of the body, not just from the brain.

It was previously thought that the hippocampus in the brain was the center for memory, because its surgical removal creates a deficit in memory. However, in 2000, Dr Eric R. Kandel received a Nobel Prize for Medicine for showing that memory resides at the level of the receptor in the cell.[61] Recent discoveries have shown that there is also a major storage area for these receptors, near the spinal chord, and that the memories are also stored throughout the bodymind.[62]

According to Dr Pert, your "molecules of emotion" mediate whether these memories are conscious or not. She highlights how "they decide what becomes a thought rising to the surface, and what remains deep in your body."[63] This means that memory is unconsciously driven by the emotions, but that it can also be made conscious by your intention.

The emotions that you're able to experience can bring recollection to the surface; if your feelings are suppressed, however, they can bury that same memory far below your awareness, where it can affect your perceptions, decisions, behavior, and even health, all unconsciously.[64]

These buried emotions make up what is often referred to by healers and psychologists as a person's "core emotional trauma." Dr Pert outlines that:

The point of therapy – including [...] energy medicine – is to bring that wound to gradual awareness, so it can be re-experienced and understood. Only then is choice possible, [...] allowing you to reintegrate any disowned parts of yourself; let go of old traumatic patterns; and become healed, or whole.[65]

EFT is both a form of energy medicine, and also the most effective way I have found so far to remove these blockages. With EFT you can release the emotional disruption that a thought or memory causes, and thus change your relationship to it. It doesn't matter whether it is a physical pain or an emotional one: once you release the blockage with EFT, both pain and emotional turmoil subside, and the results are usually permanent.

Emotional freedom

Just to clarify, freeing your emotions does not mean that you will stop experiencing what have sometimes been labeled "negative emotions." As Dr Candace Pert points out, "there are no 'bad' emotions." Emotions are problematic only when they become stuck, are not expressed, or are denied. On a biochemical level:

[I]nformation molecules get blocked at the level of the receptors, impeding the free flow of important functions throughout the psychosomatic network of the bodymind.[66]

So it is the emotional blockage, not the emotions themselves, that causes us problems. Dr Pert further asserts:

It's a misunderstanding to think that we must get rid of our dark emotions, banish them, and avoid their uncomfortable effects. They're harmful, ironically, when we resist their natural expression.[67]

So EFT will not take away your ability to express your emotions. Instead, it frees up and releases your repressed, suppressed, blocked and denied emotions, along with their related memories, which in turn affect your health and well-being.

How EFT differs from conventional talk therapies

According to Dr Candace Pert, conventional talk therapies do not include approaches that access the subconscious mind. We now know that emotion is stored throughout the body at the level of the receptor, not just in the brain. Dr Pert highlights that talk therapy addresses the mental aspects of conditions such as depression, but ignores the physical reality of such diseases, which is only half the picture.[68]

In *Molecules of Emotion*, these thoughts are echoed at a Wellness Conference by one of the presenters, David Lee:

The approach that I have trained in, traditional talk therapy, doesn't seem to impact the mind–body level. We often hear our patients say, "I know I shouldn't feel this way, but I *do!*" Knowing something doesn't always impact how we feel, and we may have to get past purely verbal communication to access our emotions.[69]

So, while talk therapy can help you process what has happened to you cognitively (in your conscious mind), it does not help you to process it energetically (in your body). It also doesn't usually access the subconscious mind. EFT, in contrast, works on the mind and body simultaneously, and also addresses the subconscious mind.

What about conventional medicine?

In the West, our over-reliance on prescription medicine has created a culture in which we do not take responsibility for our own healing. When we are sick, we tend to look outside ourselves for the answers. Dr Bruce Lipton emphasizes that:

Using prescription drugs to silence a body's symptoms enables us to ignore personal involvement we may have with the onset of the symptoms. The overuse of prescription drugs provides a vacation from personal responsibility.[70]

Dr Pert echoes these sentiments, stressing how the medical profession generally tends to focus on fixing symptoms, rather than healing the whole person:

The traditional physician doesn't talk about the toxic burden that most of us carry in our bodies, the emotional roots of trauma and stress, or how the food we eat can lead to dangerous inflammation.[71]

In contrast, Dr Pert proposes that by focusing on the bodymind, we have a new model for healing:

> [T]he paradigm of the bodymind points to new causes of disease, and [...] the many alternative therapies work to bring about deeper levels of healing than conventional medicine has come up with so far.[72]

EFT is leading this new healing movement. It enables us to take responsibility for ourselves as a whole person, and heal our traumas and emotional blockages, so that we can live in health and happiness without an over-reliance on conventional medicine.

Chapter 8

THE EFT TAPPING PROTOCOL

Please note: A diagram of the EFT tapping points can be found in Appendix 1 at the back of the book.

The following is a very basic introduction to the EFT protocol. The introduction is simple for one specific reason: all the information that you need for the EFT protocol is available for free on http://www.emofree.com – the website of EFT founder Gary Craig. On his website, Gary has generously created a free EFT manual that is available for instant download. There is also a superb tutorial that will help you to deliver the techniques skillfully and successfully. And Gary's world-renowned EFT DVDs are also available. So you can use the diagram and the information that follows to assist you in getting started right away, but for a more in-depth mastery of EFT, please visit the website.

There is also a summary of the EFT tapping protocol towards the latter part of this chapter, to help you work through it more easily. If you are new to EFT, it is advisable that you read this whole chapter a couple times, before trying EFT on yourself. And if you are using EFT specifically to work on ME, also read the chapter that follows this one, before you start.

To use EFT on yourself, first identify the issue that you want to work with. In EFT we always focus on the problem, as it is the problem that is at the heart of the energetic disruption. However, for EFT to work, you do not have to re-traumatize yourself or totally immerse yourself in the memory. In *The Healing Power of EFT* by David Feinstein, Donna Eden and Gary Craig, it is said that:

> [T]apping on acupuncture points to decrease the emotional charge around a past memory requires only that you know what you are focusing upon – clinical experience has shown that it is not necessary and it is not useful to immerse yourself in a traumatic memory or in any way retraumatize yourself for energy psychology methods to have their benefits.[73]

Therefore, you can be gentle with yourself as you resolve your issues with these techniques.

Step 1: Selecting the problem

The problem you select may be either emotional or physical. You can also work on habits of thought or patterns of behavior.

It is vital that you are specific in identifying the issue to get effective results. So if you are challenged with anxiety, then break it down into its various parts – a racing heart, a churning stomach, shortness of breath, and so on. Then deal with the parts one at a time with the EFT protocol, taking the most challenging one first.

Similarly, if you are dealing with an emotional issue such as feeling rejected, take each memory such as "The time my friend left me at the school gates," and "My father didn't come to my graduation," and again deal with them one at a time. (There will be further details on how to deal with past memories using the "Movie Technique" later in this chapter).

Step 2: Rating the problem

Give the symptom or issue that you are dealing with a number out of 10 for its intensity in the present moment, zero being not a problem and 10 being as intense as it gets. It is important to rate the problem in the present. So if you have a racing heart, how bad is it now? And if you have a memory of your father putting you down, how intense are your feelings about that memory? Giving the problem a rating helps you to see the progress that you have made during each EFT round.

Step 3: The set-up

The set-up is a way of establishing your receptiveness for change, on both a psychological and an energetic level. You may have some resistance to the change, as negative physical, emotional and behavioral energy patterns can become ingrained habits. And as highlighted in *The Healing Power of EFT*, these habits "become embedded in your energy system, your neurology and your lifestyle."[74]

In EFT, we call this resistance to change "psychological reversal." This is your unconscious resistance to the outcome you desire.

The set-up in EFT helps to overcome this reversal. This is done by either tapping on the karate chop point on the side of the hand, or rubbing on a sore spot on the left side of the chest. If you choose to tap on the karate chop point, tap on the fleshy part of the side of the hand in line with the little finger, using the tip of the index and middle fingers of the opposite hand. If you choose to rub on the sore spot, use your index and middle fingers to rub your upper chest in circular motions on the left hand side, a couple of inches across from where your arm attaches, until you find a point that is slightly sore. It is a matter of personal preference whether you choose to tap the karate chop point or rub on the sore spot. At the same time, say the set-up phrase out loud, which is "Even though I have this problem, I deeply love and accept myself." However, always replace the word *problem* with the specific symptom or issue you are working on. For example, "Even though I have this *churning stomach*, I deeply love and accept myself," or "Even though I have this *racing heart*, I deeply love and accept myself." Repeat the set-up phrase three times whilst continuing to either tap on the karate chop point or rub on the sore spot. This should diffuse the energy around any resistance to change.

The set-up is not always essential in EFT, as there is not always psychological reversal. As a newcomer, it is advisable to include it until you become familiar with the EFT protocol. As you become more experienced you can experiment with leaving it out, and see if you still get the same results.

Please note: you can alter the wording of the set-up phrase slightly to find wording that is preferable to you. Some people use "totally love and accept myself," others prefer, "deeply and profoundly love and accept myself," and some say "I'm working towards loving and accepting myself." It is a matter of personal choice, so use what feels right to you.

Step 4: The EFT sequence:
Tapping with a reminder phrase

Tapping on the EFT points will restore the flow of energy in your body's meridian system. Tap on each of the points in turn with the end of your index and middle finger (apart from when you tap on the top of the head, when you will use all four fingers of one hand). Each person has their own preferences around the pressure that they use for tapping, but ensure that you tap firmly enough to make contact with the points, but not so hard that you cause yourself physical discomfort. Tap down the body, starting from the top of the head and finishing on the karate chop point. Tap approximately seven times on each point, but it's OK if you tap more or less times on each point. Also it is fine if you accidentally miss points out in the process, so be relaxed and have fun as you learn the technique.

As you tap, use a reminder phrase to help you stay tuned into the problem. The reminder phrase is a shortened version of your set-up phrase. So if your set-up phrase was "Even though I have this churning stomach, I totally love and accept myself," your reminder phrase would be "this churning stomach."

With the exception of the points under the nose or on the chin, the EFT tapping points are on both sides of the body. You can use your left or right hand, and it doesn't matter if you tap on either side of your body, or on both sides at once. It is also OK to change sides – just go with what feels right for you.

Tap down the body, in the following sequence, repeating your reminder phrase as you tap on each point:

• First tap the top of the head on the crown with the flat of your fingers.

• Then tap the inside edge of the eyebrow, just up and across from the nose.

• Next tap the side of the eye, on the bone around the outside corner of the eye.

• Then tap the bone under the eye, about an inch below the pupil.

• Next tap under the nose, in the small hollow above the lip.

• Then tap under the bottom lip, midway between the point of the chin and the bottom of the lower lip.

• Next tap on the collar bone point. Find your collar bone and locate the U shape at the top of your breast bone, where a gentleman's tie knot would sit. At the bottom of the U shape move your fingers out one inch until you find a slight dent on either side. These are your collar bone points (also known as K-27).

• Then tap under the arm about 4 inches below the armpit. This point is approximately in line with the nipple for men and the bra strap for women.

• Optional points are found by tapping the front of your wrist with the flat of your fingers.

• Further optional points are also found on the fingers. With your palm facing you, tap the nearside corner of the thumb and each finger nail.

• Finish by tapping on the karate chop point.

This completes the EFT tapping sequence.

Step 5: The nine-gamut procedure

You can also add in another part to the technique, called the nine-gamut procedure. This is part of the classic EFT protocol, but it is not commonly used now, and it doesn't always need to be used to get brilliant results. This part of the technique helps engage and stimulate specific areas of the brain, and it can enhance the effectiveness of the procedure. It is particularly useful if you are not getting the results that you want with the basic EFT sequence of tapping with a reminder phrase. It is perhaps the most bizarre-looking aspect of the EFT protocol, with humming, counting and eye-rolling. But these processes help to engage the left and right sides of the brain, and balance the brain, which can be important for effective change.

• Place your hand on your lap. Tap on the nine-gamut point, on the back of the hand, on the dent between the ring and index finger, and continue to tap on the same point throughout the whole nine-gamut sequence.

• Now close your eyes.

• Then open your eyes.

• Whilst facing forward, look down hard to the left, and then look down hard to the right.

• Now circle your eyes 360 degrees in one direction, and then the other.

• Hum one line of a simple song, such as Happy Birthday.

• Briskly count to nine.

• Then hum again.

This completes the optional nine-gamut procedure.

Step 6: A further round of tapping

If you use the nine-gamut procedure, it is always sandwiched in between two rounds of tapping. So follow it with another round of tapping from the top of the head to the karate chop point, whilst repeating your reminder phrase.

Step 7: Reassessing the intensity of the problem

At the end of this round, check the score out of 10 to see if the intensity of your symptoms has changed. It should either have disappeared altogether or gone down. If you still have some of the problem remaining, or the intensity has gone up, continue with subsequent rounds.

Step 8: Subsequent rounds

To work on the remaining problem, start the whole procedure again. This time, adjust the set-up phrase to "Even though I still have some of this *problem*, I totally love and accept myself." As always, replace the word *problem* with a description of the symptom you are dealing with. For example "Even though I still have some of this *stomach churning*, I totally love and accept myself."

The tapping procedure is exactly the same in the following rounds, except that the word remaining is added to the beginning of the reminder phrase. So if your set-up phrase was "Even though I still have some of this stomach churning,…" your reminder phrase would be, "this remaining stomach churning."

Persist with tapping, until the symptom you are working on subsides. You can either continue with several rounds of tapping in the sequence described earlier, or vary it by including the nine-gamut procedure. If the symptom changes into something else, then start the whole procedure again, but this time rewording the set-up phrase to describe the new symptom. For example, if the stomach churning problem turns into a sinking feeling in your gut, your new set-up phrase would be "Even though I have this sinking in my gut, I totally love and accept myself." This often occurs in EFT when one symptom changes into another before it is resolved, and each shift is a sign of progress. In EFT we call this "chasing the pain," as one physical symptom resolves, and another one appears elsewhere in the body. Persist until the symptoms subside.

Step 9: Challenging the results

Once you have got the problem down to a zero, try hard to imagine the original emotion or pain, so that you can clarify that the process has worked for you. Close your eyes, and think of the problem really vividly. If there is no intensity, you know that that particular issue is resolved. If you do get some more intensity, then there is more to work on.

Step 10: Addressing different aspects and persisting

Further work may involve addressing different aspects of the problem, or more persistence on the particular issue you have been working on. Working on different aspects of the problem is sometimes fundamental to your success with EFT. The results of EFT are usually permanent, but if you haven't addressed all the aspects, it may seem like a problem has come back. So if you find that a problem is not subsiding, you may have switched to a different aspect during the process. For example, if anxiety gives you a racing heart and a churning stomach, you may need to do the EFT process on each of these to clear the anxiety. But if you accidentally switch your focus mid-process from the racing heart to the churning stomach, your results will not be as effective, and it will seem as though you have not made progress. You need to stay on each issue separately, and clear them one at a time.

Similarly, if you are working on a memory – for example, being shouted at in class – you may need to work separately on the different aspects. These could include the impact the teacher's raised voice had on you, the embarrassment of being sent outside, and then your feeling of isolation as you stood alone in the corridor. Each of these aspects may need to be addressed individually, in order to get the best results.

Likewise, if you are working on a physical problem that does not seem to shift, you might want to ask Gary Craig's favorite question on this matter: "If there was an emotional contributor to this pain, what would it be?" and then work on whatever comes up. This will help you start to look beyond the obvious, and shift the underlying cause of the problem.

Summary of the EFT protocol

Step 1 – Select the problem. Is it physical, emotional, thought-based or behavior-based? Be as specific as possible in identifying the problem.

Step 2 – Rate the problem out of 10 for how it is in this moment – 0 being not a problem and 10 being as intense as it gets.

Step 3 – Whilst tapping on the karate chop point or rubbing on the sore spot on the chest, say the set-up phrase: "Even though I have this *prob-lem*, I totally love and accept myself," replacing the word *problem* with your specific symptom or issue.

Step 4 – Tap on all the points in sequence whilst repeating a reminder phrase (a shortened version of the set-up phrase). The points are: top of the head; eyebrow; side of the eye; under the eye; under the nose; under the lower lip; on the collar bone; under the arm; plus optional points on the near side of each finger nail and across the front of wrist; and finally, finishing with the karate chop point.

Step 5 – If you wish, you can include the nine-gamut procedure. Tap on the nine-gamut point: close your eyes; open them; look down one way; look down the other; circle your eyes each way; hum; count to nine; hum again.

Step 6 – Continue with a further round of tapping using the reminder phrase.

Step 7 – Reassess the intensity of the problem with a score out of 10.

Step 8 – If the problem remains, continue with further rounds, adjusting your set-up phrase "Even though I still have some of this *problem*, I totally love and accept myself." Replace the word *problem* with the symptom or issue you are working on. Also add the word "remaining" to your reminder phrase. Persist until the problem subsides.

Step 9 – Once the problem appears to have resolved, challenge the results by trying to recreate the intensity of the original problem.

Step 10 – If there is any of the problem remaining, address different aspects of it, or persist with the original problem until it subsides. If it changes into something else, then start the procedure again with a set-up phrase which describes the new symptom.

The "Movie Technique"

To assist you in being very specific about a particular issue or event, try the "Movie Technique." Think of an issue you want to work with, then a very specific memory related to that issue. For example, the issue might be "I'm a perfectionist," and a single memory relating to this issue might be "The time my dad shouted at me when I got a low grade."

Imagine this memory is a movie and give it a title, for example "I failed." Work out how long this movie would be. If it's a short movie anywhere between several seconds or 10 minutes, then it is fine to work on it as one single movie. However, if you have hours or days worth, then break it into smaller sections where there are specific crescendos, and make each of these a separate movie.

Next, guess what the intensity of the movie would be if you ran it in your mind, but don't run it yet. Give it the usual score out of 10.

Do several rounds of tapping on the movie. For example "Even though I have this *I failed* movie, I totally love and accept myself." (Replace the words *I failed* with the title of your movie.) At the end of each round, reassess the intensity that you think the movie would be if you ran it in your mind.

When you reach the point where you no longer respond with any intensity to the thought of the movie, start running the movie through your mind or speak it out loud. Very importantly, as soon as you feel any intensity at all, stop, and tap on what ever comes up. For example, if your heart races when you remember your dad shouting at you in the movie, your set-up would simply be "Even though my heart races when I remember my dad shouting, I totally love and accept myself."

Keep running through the movie, stopping at each point that you feel any symptoms, and using the EFT protocol to deal with each symptom separately.

When you have run through the memory of the whole movie without any intensity, test it by imagining it really vividly. If you then get any intensity, clear each part with more rounds until you can remember all the events in the movie without any changes in your body chemistry.

The "Personal Peace Procedure"

This procedure was designed by Gary Craig to enable you to work on your own. Take some time to write out every negative emotional experience that you have had in your lifetime. You might want to do this in chronological order, or in the order of most to least severe experiences. Gary Craig refers to these as all your "trees in the forest," and you can use the Movie Technique to clear them one tree at a time. Try to clear one memory per day. This might take 100 days or more, but by the end you will be completely transformed. You may not need to carry out the tapping sequence for all the memories, as often when we move the intensity around major issues, other related ones become insignificant. I found clearing memories from my first 6 years to be highly beneficial.

It is also worth noting that you can work on more than one memory per day if you want to. If you are challenged with long-term illness, the sooner you clear your past traumas the quicker you are likely to heal. Gary Craig says that you can use the Personal Peace Procedure:

> …as a means to eliminate a major contributor (if not the sole cause) of a serious disease. Somewhere within one's specific events are those angers, fears and traumas that are manifesting as disease. By addressing them all, you will likely cover those responsible for the disease.[75]

However, a word of warning: if you have experienced severe trauma or have highly emotional memories, it is best to work with a qualified EFT practitioner in order to resolve them.

"Imaginary EFT"

If you are so physically tired that you are unable to carry out the EFT protocol, you can use a process called "Imaginary EFT." This involves going through the whole EFT process in your mind, without any physical tapping. You can also say the set-up and reminder phrases silently to yourself. Although this might be challenging to comprehend, it is not so remarkable. You may not be able to move a physical object such as a glass with intention, but you can move energy with intention. This technique is extremely effective for those with ME, as it means that in an energy dip not only do you have a technique that can support you, but it also gives the racing mind that often accompanies the dip something constructive to do. It is also excellent for those times when you cannot get to sleep at night, and can become an excellent and hypnotic practice if you are able to relax into it.

Using a metaphor for your physical or emotional symptoms

To help you create a very specific set-up phrase, you can use a metaphor for what it is you are feeling. This is one of my favorite ways of working with EFT, as it is very creative. Tune into the problem you are experiencing, physical or emotional. Where do you feel it in your body? What is its size? What shape is it? What texture does it have? What is its weight or density? Does it have a color? If it had a sound, what would it be?

Your set-up phrase could include any of your responses:

- "Even though I have this black, heavy tar in my heart, I love and accept myself."
- "Even though there is this burning coal in my stomach, ..."
- "Even though there are pins behind my eyes, ..."

Tap using the usual protocol and, as always, if the symptom or problem changes into something else then formulate a new set-up phrase.

Another question that you can ask yourself is: "Does this metaphor represent anything to me?" When working with clients using metaphors, I will often hear responses such as "It feels like a knife in my back," or "It feels like a fist in my stomach." My next question would be "Who do you feel stabbed you in the back," or "Whose fist is that?" The client often comes back with a very specific response. It is useful to have an EFT practitioner to ask you such questions; but if you are working on your own or with a partner, bare in mind that there may be a personal meaning behind the metaphor.

Setting goals with EFT and identifying "tail-enders"

EFT is about focusing and clearing the problem, but what about setting goals? With EFT we tap on the blocks to the goals, rather than the goals themselves. The key to effective goal-setting with or without EFT is always to be very specific. The goal "I am in good health" is too general. So set specific and achievable goals that represent the steps to good health: "I focus on a book for 10 minutes," "I walk for 2/5/10 minutes and remain energized," "I rise at 7.30am every morning," "I rest for 20 minutes two times per day." Only set one to three goals at any one time, or you will create too much pressure.

As you set each goal, give yourself a score out of 10 for how realistic the goal is for you. If it's a 6, for example, what are the blocks that are holding you back? In EFT, we call these self-limiting beliefs "tail-enders." They are the "yes, buts" that show up in your negative self-talk when you try to set a goal. Notice any tail-enders and tap them with EFT. (There are further instructions for identifying tail-enders specific to ME in Chapter 9.) "Yes, but I can't read as it gives me a headache," "Yes, but I can't walk, because it gives me leg pain," "Yes, but I can't get up first thing in the morning, as I don't sleep consistently," "Yes, but I can't rest as I feel too driven." Each tail-ender would form your set-up phrase for your goal. As part of the set-up phrase, you can also describe the emotions or feelings that arise from being blocked about your goal. For example:

• "Even though I'm so frustrated that reading gives me a headache, I totally love and accept myself."

- "Even though I get these irritating pains in my legs when I exercise, ..."

- "Even though I'm so angry that I don't sleep at night, ..."

- "Even though I'm disappointed that I feel too driven to rest, ..."

Continue to tap away all the tail-enders to achieving your goal until your belief is a solid 10 that you can reach your target. As always, persist. It might take more than one session, and there may be a multitude of aspects, related "movies," or underlying emotional issues.

Whilst you are working towards your goals, it is also useful to visualize and affirm them. Refer to Chapter 10 for more information on affirmations and goal-setting.

Persistence

You will find many stories all over the Internet about people who experience one-minute wonders with EFT. Whilst these results are impressive, do not be discouraged if you do not experience the same results instantly whilst overcoming a condition such as ME. You will need to persist with the myriad of emotional and physiological contributors to your condition. Gary Craig suggests that those who are overcoming long-term illness or serious disease tap 10–20 times per day.[76] You might want to tap when you get up, each time you visit the bathroom, and each time you fill your water glass, for example, just to remind you to get into a routine. However, as those with ME have a tendency towards self-pushing, ensure that your discipline in tapping doesn't become a means of self-punishment. Motivate yourself to tap, but don't push yourself into it if you are feeling exhausted. Also remember the "Imaginary EFT" as a substitute if you are tired.

Perceptual shifts

How will you know if EFT has worked for you? Well, apart from the obvious reduction and elimination of symptoms, you will find that you perhaps start to think about the memories or issues you have worked on in a different light. You may experience forgiveness, or at least acceptance. These will be clues to an energetic shift.

If EFT doesn't work for you

The biggest reason that EFT doesn't work for people is that they are too global about the set-up phrase. So, always remember to be as specific as possible. An example of a global set-up phrase would be "Even though I have ME, ..." A more specific set-up phrase would be "Even though I have these burning pains in my calves, ..." So always go for very specific issues or symptoms and avoid going for global problems, as they do not yield good results.

EFT should resolve your issues permanently but if they seem to come back, there may be different aspects that need addressing. So if issues seem to come back, check that you have resolved all relating past memories around a particular issue.

If EFT is still not working for you and you have persisted, then consult a qualified practitioner. In the hands of a skilled practitioner, EFT is said to have a success rate of 95% or more. If it is not working for you, it might be a matter of your technique, or you may have blocks to working on your own. If a consultation with practitioner isn't an option for you at present due to your finances, visit http://www.emofree.com for further tutorials and advice.

Chapter 9

USING EFT TO OVERCOME ME

The cycle of disease

In his highly-acclaimed *EFT For Serious Disease* training, EFT Master Karl Dawson brilliantly highlights the cycle of ME, and other similar diseases.

Karl states that this disease process starts with any negative core-beliefs that are developed in the first 6 years. These beliefs are then reinforced by upbringing and life pressures.

From this arises a tendency to negative self-talk, and stress starts to become a predominant life feature. Add to this any poor diet and lifestyle choices, plus any substance abuse or self-medication, and the cycle deepens.

From here, there is a tendency to frequent infections, colds and flu which are often tackled with antibiotics and medication. This leads to an increase in body acidity and compromising of the gut flora, where conditions such as *Candida* can then take hold.

Following this, nutrients are not easily absorbed, there is a toxic build-up, and a subsequent further debilitation of the immune system. This can lead to allergies and food intolerances.

The body then goes into constant stress, typified by an increase in HPA stimulation and adrenal burn-out. What follows is a lowered physical and mental ability to deal with life, and a worsening of symptoms.

Karl's explanation of the cycle of disease in relation to ME provides us with a very simple yet highly sophisticated explanation of what occurs in our body in the process of illness. And the good news is that with EFT, much of what has occurred can be resolved.

Working on your own versus working with a practitioner

There are many advantages to working with an EFT practitioner. Even as an advanced EFT practitioner and trainer, I still enjoy working with another practitioner if I have something that I want to resolve. Einstein famously said that "Problems cannot be solved by the same level of thinking that created them." We sometimes need someone else to lead us out of the maze that we have created for ourselves.

Working with a skilled and experienced practitioner will take you places that you are unlikely to go on your own. It will help you get to the route of issues quickly, and accelerate your healing process. Many of my clients prefer to work on their immediate symptoms on their own, and use the sessions that we have together for the deep-rooted emotional issues or traumatic memories.

However, some people also get amazing results working on their own with EFT. As mentioned earlier I experienced profound results on my EFT practitioner training course, but I also shifted the majority of my issues on my own, using the Personal Peace Procedure, and making a commitment to practice several times per day until I was well.

The following list highlights ways that you can support your recovery from ME with EFT. This list has been divided into two halves: things you could try on your own; and things you will probably need a practitioner to help you with. Of course, you may prefer to work solely with a practitioner, but if you are on a budget, it helps to know what you can feasibly tackle on your own and what you might need help with.

The list is only a guideline, so use your own judgment, and work carefully at a pace that suits you. And as always, you can use EFT on your own, but be sensible, and consult a practitioner if you have deep emotional scars that should not be handled without assistance.

Things to try on your own with EFT

Managing symptoms

You can use EFT on your physical or emotional symptoms. This is something that you can do on your own as a newcomer to EFT. Tune into each symptom separately and follow the EFT protocol to resolve each problem in turn. For example, "Even though I have this foggy brain, I deeply and completely love and accept myself," or "Even though I have this pain in my calves, I deeply and profoundly love and accept myself." Some symptoms may need persistence, and you might need to find the root emotional cause, either on your own or with a practitioner. But in the meantime, EFT is a great tool for helping you to reduce physical and emotional discomfort in your daily life.

Approaching your symptoms through metaphor

Gary Craig suggests that you tap on your symptoms through metaphor.[77] Describe how you think ME looks inside your body, and use the description as a set-up phrase:

- "Even though it feels like battery acid down my nervous system, I totally love and accept myself."
- "Even though my calves feel like lead, ..."
- "Even though there is cotton wool in my brain, ..."

This is a creative way to tune into and shift your symptoms.

Clearing emotional issues around the illness

Long-term illness is often accompanied by a whole host of emotional issues. These can include: feeling devalued as you are not able to financially contribute; financial fears; feeling socially isolated; lowered self-esteem due to loss of status; and so on. You can use EFT to clear these feelings one by one. You may need a practitioner to help you do this, but if you want to tackle it on your own, take one issue at a time.

There are two things you can do. The first is to tune into the feeling that this issue gives you, describe where you feel that feeling in your body, and follow the EFT protocol. For example, if you have financial worries, and this creates a sinking in your heart, then the sinking feeling is what you would work with. Your set-up phrase might be "Even though I have this sinking heart when I think about my finances, I totally love and accept myself." There might be more than one symptom for each issue.

Tapping on the feelings will help you manage and resolve the symptoms related to the issue, but to clear the root cause, the second thing you can do is to tap on separate memories relating to each issue, using the Movie Technique. Examples for financial worries might include memories from your childhood of seeing your mum panic when there wasn't enough money, or comments people might have made to you about your inability to contribute. Each memory is a separate aspect that may be contributing to your distress, and each time you clear a memory it will bring you closer to personal peace.

Clearing blockages around the original triggers to your condition

In order to heal, it is vital to clear your relationship to any stress that might have occurred at the onset of the illness. Even if your condition was triggered by a virus or a vaccination, it is very common to find that there was also a huge amount of personal stress that preceded the illness, and EFT can help to clear this. For myself, and many of the clients I have worked with, there has been a story of an uncommon amount of personal stress at the start of the condition. There has also often been a "last straw" event, where the person felt as though their life was hanging together by a thread and then one more stressful event sent them spiraling into illness. This is often the time that the initial virus struck, from which they never quite felt they had recovered.

Think back to the start of the illness and remember the stresses that you might have been under at that time. Does thinking about them change your body chemistry? Do you get a sinking feeling, a racing heart, a lump in your throat, a dip in energy, a sense of panic, a feeling of dread, or something similar? If you do, use the Movie Technique to deal with the memories around the start of your illness, one at a time.

Using EFT to identify and overcome tail-enders

In his brilliant *EFT for Serious Disease* tutorial, Gary Craig suggests that you imagine yourself in perfect health and then tap away any tail-enders, (the "yes, buts" that prevent you reaching your goal).[78] So picture yourself in perfect health, then describe the resistances you experience. The following are a selection of examples from my clients.

I see myself in perfect health, but if I get better:

- "...it would mean I have to go out in the world."
- "...I would have to manage my energy."
- "...I would have to go back to my job, and I always hated it."
- "...I wouldn't have any time to myself."

Whatever comes up for you, transform it into a set-up phrase. For example, "Even though I'm afraid of going back out in the world, I totally love and accept myself." Remember, there is no judgment here, and everyone's tail-enders might be different. So see this as an experiment in what is blocking you, rather than a means of being harsh on yourself.

Things to work through with a qualified EFT practitioner

You will find a number of EFT practitioners who can help you with the following issues. Fortunately EFT can be practiced over the telephone, so you can work with a practitioner from anywhere in the world. It is preferable, but not essential, to find one who has experience of working with your condition, or with other long-term illness. An increasing number of EFT practitioners have undergone Karl Dawson's *EFT for Serious Disease* training, and this focuses on ME in some detail. However, there are also many brilliant EFT practitioners who have not undergone this training, so if you find someone that feels right for you, then go with your instincts.

Clearing the emotions around childhood or life trauma

EFT can help you clear the emotions around past traumas, that may be lowering your emotional threshold and weakening your immune system. When we experience a trauma, a part of us splits off and disassociates. Often we can't remember what has happened, while on another level we are reliving the traumatic event over and over again in our subconscious mind. EFT can help you heal parts of yourself that may still be disassociated. Working with an EFT practitioner, you can change your relationship to any childhood or life trauma that might be contributing to your condition.

By far the most effective way I have experienced doing this is by using a technique created by Karl Dawson which he has named "Matrix Reimprinting." This involves an adaptation of the Movie Technique, and you may need a practitioner to guide the process. Karl explains that there are "echoes" of our past selves in our energy fields, and these are often a result of unresolved trauma from the past. Using Karl's brilliant technique, you would run the movie as you remember it. At an appropriate place in the movie, the practitioner would stop you, and tap on you, whilst you imagined tapping on the younger version of yourself. You could then enter into a dialog with your younger self, asking what life messages you got from the particular situation, and if there is anything you need to help you in that situation. Also, with all the knowledge and the wisdom that you have now, you can reassure your younger self, and help them gain a new perspective. The younger version of yourself could then change the outcome of the movie. This allows you to express yourself differently in the past situation.

This technique is tremendously therapeutic. It obviously doesn't change the past, but it changes your relationship to it completely. It changes the pictures in your mind and energy field, and ultimately the way you relate to those pictures. And when you re-run the old movie afterwards, it completely changes your feelings towards it.

You may need to find an EFT practitioner who has trained with Karl in order to experience Matrix Reimprinting. Alternatively you can view this technique on Karl Dawson's *EFT for the Prevention and Treatment of Serious Diseases* DVD set. I can honestly say that this technique has had an incredible transformational effect on my life, and I use it to great effect in all my sessions with clients. However, you can still get great results with the traditional Movie Technique, which is also an extremely quick and powerful way of overcoming your childhood or life traumas.

Addressing and changing negative core beliefs

In his *EFT for Serious Disease* training, Karl Dawson highlights how wrong core beliefs, which are usually formed from our experiences in our first 6 years, can contribute to poor health and disease. This is because wrong core beliefs create stress, and stress creates illness. A few example that Karl gives are "I must be perfect to be loved," "People must think well of me," "I must be in control," "I'm unlovable," and so on. If we are running these core beliefs, they influence how we think, feel and behave on every level. You can identify and overcome these beliefs using EFT.

There may be a whole host of experiences and memories contributing to these core beliefs, and it is likely that you will need a practitioner to help you to identify and overcome them, as they often run very deep. You may also need a whole series of sessions around one core belief. If you do choose to work on your own with core beliefs, a good way to assess your progress is to use the Validity of Cognition (VOC) scale. If your core belief is that you are unlovable, what percentage do you believe this, with 0% being "It's totally untrue" and 100% being "It is totally true"? Make a note. Then, as you work on all the separate memories throughout your life that contributed to this belief, make a note of how your VOC scale changes. If you believe that you are 95% unlovable, and you deal with a memory that takes this score down to 90%, this represents huge progress. Equally, you may be surprised to discover one key memory that was creating this belief, and your score may drop dramatically in just one session.

Gary Craig refers to these negative core beliefs as "the writing on our walls." For more information on addressing core beliefs using EFT, see Gary's brilliant, free download entitled *The Palace of Possibilities*.[79]

Addressing and changing blocking beliefs

Many people also have what Karl Dawson terms "blocking beliefs" about their illness. These can include notions such as "I am being punished for something in a previous lifetime," "God would heal me if he really loved me," "The doctor said I would always be on medication," "I have attracted this illness to overcome it for others' benefit," and so on.

Beliefs specific to ME may include "Not everyone makes a full recovery from ME," "I've been ill too long to get better," "I'm too old to get fully well," "I've always been sickly," etcetera.

If these are deep-rooted beliefs, you might need to do some detective work to figure out where they came from, and do some further tapping. For example, if you believe you have always been sickly you can make a list of all the illnesses you have experienced, and tap through each one with the Movie Technique. You can also tap on any memories you have about being told by others that you are sickly. For example: "Even though my mum once said I was a sickly child, I totally love and accept myself," or "Even though my boss said I have the worst sickness record in the company, I totally love and accept myself."

You may need a practitioner to help you identify any blocking beliefs, as they can be so ingrained that you don't even realize you are running them.

Addressing the issues at the heart of your illness

There are often underlying issues or themes in any illness. Although everybody's healing journey is unique to them, there are some common themes that run through ME, such as perfectionism and being highly driven. You may have been told you are a "type A" personality or that it's just the way you are. But you only behave in that way because of your upbringing and conditioning. So with some detective work using EFT, you can determine what life experiences contributed to these beliefs and move through them.

Addressing and changing self-sabotaging behaviors

You can use EFT to help you overcome any self-sabotaging behaviors that may be affecting your healing. Common ones for ME can include: pushing yourself until you drop; not allowing yourself adequate rest or relaxation; ignoring signals from your body that it is time to stop; and eating foods that you might be intolerant to. Again, EFT can help you address what is actually driving you to behave in this way, and to switch from being driven to being positively and appropriately motivated.

These self-sabotaging behaviors are usually a result of unconscious messages we have received from life experiences. For example, if your parents always worked very long hours and did not award themselves breaks, this can become a normalized behavior. By contrast, it might be that you were praised as a child only when you worked really hard. Of course, these are very simplified examples and the truth is usually much more complex, with a myriad of life messages that have reinforced your behavior. This is why it can help to have a practitioner to support you in getting to the root of some of the more complex issues.

Personally, my own self-sabotaging behaviors were around not wanting to stop and face myself. I pushed myself really hard as a way of blocking my emotions from the trauma I had experienced. But I was also addicted to achieving, and was very goal-orientated. My wounded inner child still needed certificates and praise by way of verification that she was a good person. All this was resolved through EFT, and I have to think really hard now to remember the person who pushed through the pain to get things done!

Addressing secondary gains

For many, there are underlying benefits to remaining ill. We are not always aware of these, and there is no blame if we are running these programs, as they are often unconscious. These behaviors are known as secondary gains. A secondary gain is when there is some external pay-off for remaining ill, and secondary gains are common to all types of illness.

For some, illness is the only way that they get rest or attention. I have so many clients who have lived their lives at 100 miles an hour, and the illness is almost a welcome break. It means that they get care or attention, and no longer have to continue with a multitude of duties.

Others see the world as a frightening and dangerous place, and illness keeps them protected as they do not have to go out alone, or face stressful situations. Their main care-giver, with the best intentions, often colludes with them to keep them safe.

Others are so identified with their problem that they cannot imagine life without it. They may be a member of meeting or campaign groups, and have a large number of friends with the same condition.

You may or may not be aware of any gains that are keeping you from healing, but if you have them they can be addressed in a non-judgmental manner using EFT. If you feel angered by what you have just read, there is a good chance that you have an underlying secondary gain. If you are doing this work on your own, ask yourself "What are my pay-offs for having this condition?" Be honest with yourself.

To help you feel less judged or defensive, I shall share the secondary gain I overcame. Before I became ill with ME I had a large debt, which I had accumulated when I had the salary to pay it. When I became ill with ME, I could not pay it, and the threatening letters I received had added to my symptoms and escalated my condition. I was a nervous wreck every time the phone rang or a letter came, to the point where I could no longer answer the phone or read my own mail. Finally, after 8 months of poor advice from a debt management agency, and lots of negotiation by my partner, I was exempt from dealing with the debt until I was well.

So somewhere deep in my subconscious, I had decided that it was safer to remain ill, as it kept me from having to deal with the turmoil and stress that I associated with the debt. Of course, this decision was not made consciously; nevertheless, it was keeping me from healing. It was only by doing some clever detective work with EFT that I realized and resolved the issue. I used the Movie Technique to tap on all my memories around debt collectors and banks, and also around all my memories of financial problems that we had in my childhood. This resolved the secondary gain issue that was preventing me from healing.

Using EFT to work with allergies and sensitivities

Allergies and sensitivities are a complex issue, and they often accompany ME. They are definitely not my area of expertise, and I am not qualified as an allergy specialist. I can, however, offer what I have learned and observed about allergies over the years.

The pattern I usually hear from my clients who are overcoming ME is that several years before their condition started, they gradually became intolerant to wheat, dairy, yeast, caffeine, alcohol, sugar, additives, and so on. Chemical sensitivities also often develop, followed by dust allergies, and for some, even bottled water can cause physical upset. In fact, while I still had ME, I was amazed to hear from friends who had the condition, that they had this same spiraling of intolerances several years *before* the onset of the condition. This very fact is what started me on an exploration of what lies beneath the illness. Of course, now that I have studied EFT, and the *Serious Disease* course with Karl Dawson, I understand that these allergies were part of the cycle of disease. But if you are still attached to the idea that a single virus caused your condition, the fact that the allergies usually start long before the initial virus for many people, might help you to question this theory.

I had over 20 food allergies when I had ME. When I was at my most ill, I could tolerate only meat and green vegetables. For some time, every other food that I ate – including organic eggs, potatoes, carrots, grains, and fruit – gave me black and red, swollen eyes and severe pains in my abdomen. When I turned up at my EFT training, and had to stay in self-catering facilities so that I could eat while I was there, EFT

Master Karl Dawson asked, "The world's a dangerous place then, is it, Sasha?" What Karl understood is that allergies can be a metaphor for the danger we perceive in the world. In a certain fear-based mind-set, everything can be poisonous.

When Karl said this to me, my first thought was "That's not fair!" However, it was closely followed by a second thought which was, "But yes, he's right, the world *is* a dangerous place. I *do* believe that!" And interestingly, when I changed this belief with EFT (and PSYCH-K®), my allergies went away.

There are numerous suggestions to the origins of allergies in ME. One suggestion is that with ME, the immune system becomes hyper-vigilant and turns against the food we eat. Another is that a compromising of gut flora (where up to 85% of the immune response is said to take place) causes leaky gut, meaning that food substances pass through the gut wall into the blood.

I have also heard anecdotes of people who have been eating a certain food substance when they have heard tragic or distressing news, and they have since become intolerant to that food. The body learns to associate a stress response with that food, and assumes that the food is the cause. For those with ME, this could offer another explanation of why there are so many intolerances associated with the condition. If you are in a constant stress state due to the overactive hypothalamus, the body could be continuously re-triggering the subconscious belief that the food is the causative agent.

The expert in allergies in the field of EFT is Sandi Radomski. She has developed a process called Allergy Antidotes™. Sandi's three-step process is as follows:

(1) Assess whether substance sensitivities are a possible cause of

symptoms;

(2) Identify specific reactive substances;

(3) Use energy psychology techniques to reprogram the body to no longer react negatively to the reactive substances.

Sandi outlines that in step 3:

[T]he patient holds the substance, or holds a tube with the energetic signature of the substance, or holds a piece of paper with the name of the substance, or says or thinks about the substance. By stimulating acupuncture points, we eliminate the energy imbalance in relation to that substance, thereby ending the body's negative reaction.[80]

These techniques may calm the disruption in your energy system in relation to the item you are intolerant to. Sandi's manual can be ordered from her website http://www.allergyantidotes.com, which will teach you to work with these techniques more specifically. You can also find Sandi on the *EFT Speciality Series 2* DVDs.[81] However, an important word of warning: do *not* experiment with these techniques if you have anaphylactic or strong reactions to certain foods or substances. This is because if you carry out EFT on an allergic condition, it can re-trigger the allergic response *without* the food being ingested, or the substance being present. As always, seek professional help for your medical conditions.

Important note on the use of EFT:

Feeling worse before you feel better

People usually make excellent progress with EFT, but be aware that occasionally you may feel worse before you feel better. There are a number of reasons for this. Firstly, you are removing blockages in your energy system, and redistributing energies around your body. Also, you are detoxifying long-standing emotional issues. Furthermore, you are releasing destructive behaviors and thought patterns that may have been with you for some time. As a result, some people with ME feel more fatigued at the start of using EFT, as their energies redistribute. If this happens to you, don't let it discourage you from continuing. Remember, in the long run the results are likely to be worth a short period of increased fatigue. So, see it as a good sign as something is obviously changing within you, keep tapping, and consult a practitioner if you need further guidance.

Using EFT with the "25% group"
A note for practitioners and care-givers

There is a proportion of the ME population who are severely disabled with the condition. This group is often referred to as the "25% group," as approximately a quarter of those with ME fall into this category, going on to develop severely debilitating symptoms that can last for years. EFT is still equally beneficial in these circumstances, but there are some careful considerations if you are using EFT with a member of this group.

Firstly, a number of this group are completely bed-bound, in extreme pain, and with noise and light sensitivity. Some lie in darkened rooms, wearing dark glasses. These symptoms are very real physiological symptoms. So if you are either an EFT practitioner called upon to work with a client in this situation, or a care-giver of someone in this situation, you will need to be very delicate with the EFT procedure. Most importantly, please ensure you have the client's consent to practice. Also, check if there are any legal considerations to working with this client group in your state, province or country.

From my experience with some of the more extreme cases, I found the best approach was to start by very gentle and light touching of the points, barely making contact at all. Even extremely light touch can be very painful for the recipient, so please be aware and set up a method of communication with your client.

At the start, gently making contact with the points may be best carried out without a set-up statement at all, if your client is very noise-sensitive or has difficulty verbalizing and communicating. You would expect to work in this way for about 10 minutes, during which time the client may need breaks. It is likely that you will need to talk in hushed tones or whispers, if at all. If you are a practitioner, then the best use of your time may be to train the main care-giver to work in this way. The care-giver could start with one round per day, building up to several rounds per day over the next month, and eventually increasing to ten rounds or more per day, if the client is willing. This must be introduced slowly so as not to induce an extreme healing reaction in the client, which is more likely with this group.

As an EFT practitioner you may be keen to get to the core issues as soon as possible. This is not recommended! You need to exercise extreme patience with this client group, taking time for their body's energy system to release some of the intense physiological disruption, before you start to deal with the underlying emotional causes. Please proceed slowly with extreme caution, and only take on such a case if you are qualified, experienced, confident, and insured to do so.

Most of all, be sensitive to the needs of the client, and do not assume that you know what is best for them, or try to project onto them what you think they might need. Expect slow progress, but celebrate any improvement, however small it may seem. The fact that your client managed to turn themselves over in bed or reach for their own glass of water could be a huge achievement for them. Remember that they may have been in this situation for a number of years (sometimes even decades), and that any small step forward that they make is going to be highly beneficial. As we know, EFT is an astonishing tool, and used correctly with this group, it could help to completely transform their lives.

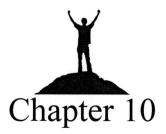

Chapter 10

OTHER THINGS YOU CAN DO TO SUPPORT YOUR HEALING

The following are suggestions, in no particular order, of other things you can do to reinforce your healing. Many of them apply to any health condition, not just to ME. You won't need to do them all in order to heal, and certain things may resonate more with you than others, so celebrate your uniqueness and go with what feels right for you. Also, it is advisable not to try and do them all at once, or you will create more pressure for yourself, which will work against the healing process. All the books and products mentioned below can be found in the resources section of this book, or on my website http://www.bodymindhealing.co.uk. Also, many of the suggestions and techniques presented below can be enhanced with the use of EFT.

Accept the illness

This is the starting point of your recovery, and is very different from giving in to the illness. Try and move away from Western thinking, which uses lots of war metaphors in relation to illness, and talks of fighting it. You do not need to fight in order to recover. If you perceive yourself as fighting your illness, you can create further stress. Try and stop thinking back to the past and longing for how things used to be, or going forward into the future longing to be anywhere else but here. Instead, treat your illness as your teacher: it is showing you what you need to change about yourself in order to be well. If you are having trouble accepting where you are, read *Loving What Is* by Bryon Katie, or visit her website http://www.thework.com. Use EFT to tap away any resistance you may have to acceptance of your current condition.

Use positive language

In order to heal, change how you think and talk about ME. Instead of referring to yourself as someone who is "suffering" from ME, refer to yourself as someone who is "recovering" from ME. Changing the messages you give to yourself and others about your healing will affect your ability to heal. This applies to any health condition, not just to ME.

This is crucial because the mind and body are one, and according to Dr Candace Pert, what you think and say has a direct impact on the state of your cells. Your spleen, lymph nodes and immune cells are in close communication with your brain. And Dr Pert explains that if you say the words "I have a bad knee," for example, it is as though you push a button in your brain that keeps reproducing painful symptoms. However, if you tell yourself "My body heals," then Dr Pert explains that you will redirect the inflammatory immune cells away from the joint, and the condition can cease to exist.[82]

Live in "soft time"

In her inspirational book *Pure Bliss,* Gill Edwards outlines the difference between living in "hard time" and "soft time".[83] Soft time is that wonderful way of being that feels very gentle and present. It is the state in which we enjoy the simple pleasures in life and experience bliss. For those living in soft time, tasks are completed in "flow time," where there is a sense of joy in undertaking activities. When you are living in the soft-time/flow-time cycle, you gently move between rest and activity in a balanced way, enjoying the contrast between being and doing.

The opposing cycle is what Gill calls "hard time". In this cycle, there is a sense of busyness and effort in everything you do. In hard time, you feel driven, anxious and obligated. This cycle often leads to martyrdom and guilt. You may clock-watch or feel pressured. It seems that your tasks lack meaning and that your life becomes a series of tick-boxes as you strive for an indefinable goal. This treadmill approach invariably leads to exhaustion, stress and burnout. In hard-time cycles, recovery time is referred to as "lost time," as there is a need to escape through joyless pursuits. This leads us to feelings of emptiness and frustration, and a tendency to search outside ourselves for happiness.

In my own personal experience of overcoming ME, and in the work that I have done with countless clients, I have found that almost everyone recovering from ME has been living in the hard-time cycle. This is evident in what is traditionally known as the "boom-and-bust" cycle, where as soon as there is a small amount of energy, those over-coming ME go straight into busyness until they crash again. By resolving the underlying causes of this cycle with EFT, and working out your subconscious motivation for pushing yourself like this, you can switch into a soft-time cycle more easily.

Take a naturopathic perspective on healing

In naturopathy, all healing is self-healing, and the body can heal itself if given the right circumstances. Presumably, if you are reading this book, you are already taking responsibility for your health. But I have also met many people who are waiting for someone to invent a magic pill so that they can recover from ME. If this has been the case for you, then let's hope you are beginning to shift your thinking. Your body has amazing restorative powers if you give it what it needs in order to heal.

A naturopathic approach would include following nature's laws by getting the right amount of rest and sleep, eating natural and organic foods, drinking plenty of water, getting sunlight on the skin for vitamin D, getting some form of appropriate exercise, relaxation, and so on.

Release your anger about the injustice surrounding ME

Yes, those who have been challenged with ME have encountered a great deal of prejudice about their condition. The problem is that many of those in recovery get very attached to this injustice. However, focusing on it will not enhance your healing potential; in fact, it will hamper it.

At the start of the illness, I was very much attached to the injustice I had encountered. I joined news groups and read countless stories of the suffering of others – and I suffered with them. I let myself be bombarded with emails that often brought me to tears. But did this help me heal? Not in the slightest. In fact, it worsened my condition. And it wasn't until I let it go that I started to heal.

So if you must be involved in helping others to overcome their misconceptions about the condition, write a letter, sign a campaign, or make a positive contribution, then let it go. Anger will only trigger adrenaline and keep you in a cycle of poor health. Use EFT to tap away any frustration you have about the injustice you have been feeling. Use the Movie Technique to focus on one issue at a time, such as visits to doctors and medical examinations. Similarly, work on individual memories of things that other people have said to you about your condition, based on their misperceptions.

Surround yourself with positive, healthy people

We are vibrational beings and we pick up on each other's energy. If you want to be in good health, surround yourself with those who are in the vibration of good health. If you do feel the need to have friends who are overcoming ME, the worst thing you can do is talk about your symptoms. Focusing on illness is not going to create health. You will simply keep each other in a lower vibration and reflect the illness back to each other. If you want to have friends who have ME, make sure they are people who take a solution-focused approach to their recovery. Share information and knowledge, celebrate your progress, cheer each other on, make each other laugh, and practice EFT together. This way you will be reinforcing each other's healing, rather than reinforcing the illness. But always put your own health first. You are your biggest priority.

Learn about and apply the "Law of Attraction"

This law is governed by quantum physics. It is based on the understanding that we are all connected in a unified energy field, and it states that what we focus on is what we get. It has been popularized by the film *The Secret*, and in that same film there are interviews with a number of remarkable people, who have used the Law of Attraction to overcome extreme medical conditions such as cancer and paralysis. The film is highly recommended, as are books by Esther and Jerry Hicks. For a related EFT book on this subject, read *Attracting Abundance with EFT*, by Carol Look.

Learn to climb your emotional scale

In their inspiring book *Ask and it is Given*, Esther and Jerry Hicks present the Teachings of Abraham. A key component of these teachings is the emotional scale, which is a way of monitoring and changing your alignment with Source Energy. The emotional scale is outlined in *Ask and it is Given* as follows:

1 – Joy, knowledge, empowerment, freedom, love, appreciation;

2 – Passion;

3 – Enthusiasm, eagerness, happiness;

4 – Positive expectation, belief;

5 – Optimism,

6 – Hopefulness;

7 – Contentment;

8 – Boredom;

9 – Pessimism;

10 – Frustration, irritation, impatience;

11 – "Overwhelment";

12 – Disappointment;

13 – Doubt;

14 – Worry;

15 – Blame;

16 – Discouragement;

17 – Anger;

18 – Revenge;

19 – Hatred, rage;

20 – Jealousy;

21 – Insecurity, guilt, unworthiness;

22 – Fear, grief, depression, despair, powerlessness.[84]

As you probably already know, it is not within the realms of most people's capabilities to jump from depression to joy. But the Teachings of Abraham highlight how you can move up your emotional guidance scale, by consciously reaching for a feeling that is improved from the one you are presently experiencing. So if you are feeling angry about your condition, try reaching for a feeling that is just above this, such as doubtfulness that you will ever heal. From here, you might feel disappointed that you can't do all the things you used to do. You could turn this feeling into frustration that it is taking you so long to get better. You could then tune into the boredom that you feel about your condition. Then it is just a small step up from feeling contented that you have come quite a long way in your healing process. This contentment could turn to hopefulness as you realize that since you have come so far, there is every reason that you could fully recover. So hopefulness could turn to optimism. Then, as you read more about others that have recovered, and begin to make positive changes to your lifestyle, you might move into belief in your ability to heal. You might then jump right up to appreciation as you draw all the right things into your path to ensure your healing.

There is no set time for how long you spend in each stage. You might be able to move up in minutes, hours, days, or weeks. The important thing is to reach for a feeling that is higher than the one you are currently experiencing, and to aim to keep moving up. If it is anger, for example, express it, then let it go. However, although it is not part of the Teachings of Abraham, I have found using EFT to be an incredibly fast way of moving up the emotional scale. For example:

- "Even though I have this sinking doubt that I'll never get better, I totally love and accept myself."
- "Even though I'm frustrated with my condition, ..."
- "Even though I'm so bored of feeling like this, ..." etc.

Experiment and enjoy no longer being a victim of your emotions. Further detail on working with the emotions can be found in *The Astonishing Power of Emotions*, by Esther and Jerry Hicks.

Journal your progress

Effective journaling is about reflecting on what has gone well, and also identifying your patterns so that you can move through them. Use your journal to record your successes in EFT, and highlight when you have slipped into unhelpful or self-sabotaging behaviors, so that you can change them. Do this in a positive and solution-focused way, and never use your journal as a way to undermine or discredit yourself. You are doing your absolute best in every moment, and reflecting on your progress will help you define your success.

One error I made when I was journaling whilst overcoming ME was to have a section in my journal entitled "One thing I could have done better today." It was pointed out to me that this was a fault-finding exercise, which meant that I was looking for a way to criticize myself. I change this to "The best thing I did today," and I started to feel immediately better about myself. Sometimes we need to lighten up in order to give ourselves the best chance of healing.

Have a "Glad of the Day"

Each day, focus on something positive that happened, and celebrate it. You can also make a list of all the things you are glad about. The smallest things can go on your list. The fact that someone was kind to you. The fact that you received a nice email. The fact that the sun came out. Only include positives on your list. This will raise your energy and your vibration. Tap away any negatives in your day using EFT.

Make a "Well Done Me!" list

Make a list of all the things you have achieved in your life. Keep adding to it daily as you achieve even the smallest of goals. This will help you stay focused on the positive and feel good about your progress.

Balance your life

Many people who are overcoming ME are uncomfortable with the word "pacing." If you have heard this word one too many times, try replacing it with the word "balancing." We all need to lead a balanced life in order to be healthy, so work towards putting the balance back in your life on a daily basis. If your life has been unbalanced for so long that you are not even sure what a balanced life would look like, you might want to invest in some sessions with a life coach, or a book on life coaching, such as Fiona Harrold's *Be Your Own Life Coach*, or Cheryl Richardson's *Take Time For Your Life*.

A word of warning, though: if you do decide to coach yourself, make sure that you have small, realistic and achievable goals. Be sure that this doesn't become another way of putting pressure on yourself. Some people respond well to time-framed goals, and almost everybody responds to writing down their achievements, and reviewing their setbacks.

A great tool from life coaching to help you become more balanced is to assess yourself in terms of the different areas of life:

- Finance/work/education
- Family
- Relationships
- Spirituality
- Health and well-being
- Environment
- Personal growth
- Fun and recreation

If all these areas were in balance, then in theory, your life would flow smoothly. But certain areas get neglected and others over-emphasized. Using tools from coaching, you can work out which aspects are being overlooked and work towards small and achievable goals in one to two areas of your life at a time. Don't become too attached to your goals, though. They are there to help you improve your life, and not for your inner pusher to put more pressure on.

Have some fun

This could be one of the most important things you can do to heal. Overcoming illness can become a grind if you let it, so try to connect regularly with the things that fill you with joy. The best medicine is laughter, which will increase your endorphin levels and enhance your immunity. Watch and listen to comedy – either live or recorded. Fill your life with joy at every opportunity. Tap away any resistance to joy, or any negative beliefs that fun is not important.

Also engage in playful activities with others. If you need more convincing about the importance of this, consider what neuroscientist Candace Pert says about play in *Everything You Need to Know to Feel Good*:

> [P]lay is more than simple stress-reduction. [...] When we are playing, we are stretching our emotional expressive ranges, loosening up our biochemical flow of information, getting unstuck, and healing our feelings.[85]

She also outlines how:

> Having fun is the cheapest, easiest and most effective way [...] to instantly reduce stress and rejuvenate mind, body and spirit. The source of most people's ongoing daily stress [...] is the perception of isolation and alienation, being cut off from the company of others. Engaging in play is the antidote because it gets our emotions flowing, and our emotions are

what connect us, give us a sense of unity, a feeling that we are part of something greater than our small and separate egos.[86]

So, as you recover, remember to prioritize fun as a part of your healing journey.

Adopt a spiritual perspective

According to author and spiritual teacher William Bloom, enhancing your spiritual connection will also increase your endorphin levels. You do not need to be associated with any particular religious group to do this. You might want to spend some time appreciating nature, meditating, or just having some quiet time to reconnect with the joy of living. If you have blocks to spirituality, you can tap them away too.

Learn present-moment awareness

The majority of our problems come from focusing on the past or fearing the future. Learning present-moment awareness is perhaps a lifetime challenge for us in the Western world, and is best seen as a practice rather than an end goal. Every time you catch yourself thinking about the past or future, just gently bring yourself back to the present. Using EFT to clear past memories will also assist you in being here more often. And learning meditation is a great way to develop present-moment awareness.

Invest in the *Holosync* program

This incredible tool will help you to:

- achieve meditation;
- positively influence your brain-wave patterns;
- reduce your stress levels, by increasing DHEA;
- reduce your cortisol levels, which in turn will decrease stress;
- increase melatonin, which will aid sleep.

It is worth the investment and its results are quick and lasting. Visit http://www.bodymindhealing.co.uk for more information.

Invest in biofeedback software for your computer

This will help you to understand the mind–body connection. Highly recommended is the *Healing Rhythms* software, which contains:

- games to help you relax and be present;
- breathing and present-moment awareness exercises from leading spiritual teachers;
- a biofeedback monitor, which will assist you to slow down your heart rate and make it more coherent.

Again, an excellent investment, if you are not too affected by sitting in front of a computer for a short while. Visit http://www.bodymindhealing.co.uk for more information.

Learn deep relaxation

Many people who are overcoming ME find it challenging to relax due to the over-stimulation of the sympathetic nervous system that accompanies the condition. Deep relaxation takes you out of the fight-or-flight state, and enables you to slow your heart rate and adrenals. Relaxation also releases endorphins, which will facilitate healing. Practice relaxation two or three times daily for 20–30 minutes, to maximize your healing potential.

Try this exercise, adapted from *Recovery Yoga*[87] by Sam Dworkis. Ensure you are in a warm and comfortable room with no distractions. You might prefer to put on some soothing music to help you relax. Lay on your back on a comfortable surface, preferably other than your bed. Put a pillow under your knees and head, and cover your body and eyes. You might want to try tensing and relaxing each muscle in turn, starting at your feet and working up to your head. Then try some deep breathing, with the aim of allowing your abdomen to rise and fall as you do. Take ten deep breaths. Then a further ten breaths, slowing your out-breath only. Followed this with a further ten breaths, slowing your in-breath only. Then a final ten breaths slowing both your in- and out-breath.

Try to keep an empty mind as you do this. It will not be as effective if you are laying there making your shopping list or deciding what you are going to do next. But be patient with yourself, as relaxation is a skill that is learned through practice. You may benefit from having a one-off session with a yoga teacher who understands your condition, in order to learn to relax fully.

Affirm your health

Popularized by the brilliant and inspirational Louise Hay, affirmations about health will help you increase your vibration of health.

According to Dr Candace Pert:

[Y]our words and thoughts strengthen synaptic connections in your brain, changing your neural patterns, or networks, giving you a personal experience of reality and potentially bringing about the results you want. Spoken words – either positive or negative – have the power to create a reality you either want or don't.[88]

So, affirm as though health is already yours. Examples of affirmations to increase health include "My body heals itself," "I always expect brilliant health," "I love my body," "I am safe and calm as my body heals," "Every day in every way my body heals more and more," "I enjoy taking care of myself, ""My health is my birthright," and so on.

Use EFT to tap away any resistance or "tail-enders" to the affirmations. Always say the affirmation in present tense, as though what you want has already occurred. Avoid saying "I will" or "I want," as they are future-focused and will not bring the same results as if you say the affirmation as though it is true in the present. Also, say it like you mean it and believe it, while at the same time allowing yourself to feel the affirmation as you say it. Practice several times a day if you can.

Visualize your health

Visualization is another powerful tool for your healing. It has been used to help people reduce tumors, and heal a whole host of conditions that were previously thought to be incurable without medical intervention. Though it may sound strange, this is not so remarkable now that we are starting to understand the power of the mind to heal the body.

Close your eyes and relax. Then simply visualize certain parts of your body healing. For example, you may visualize your hypothalamus functioning effectively, your nervous system soothing, or your heart rhythm stabilizing. Alternatively, picture your whole being in vibrant health. At the same time as you visualize, allow the feeling of health to flow through you. Practice this often to enhance your healing.

Get the right nutrition and supplementation

You might need some help to determine what is right for you. I am not a nutritionist, but the following recommendations are fairly universal for those overcoming ME. VegEPA help to overcome the essential fat deficiency that accompanies ME, and are available in the UK at a discounted price for those overcoming ME. Juice Plus increases your antioxidant level. Zeolite will help clear heavy metals from your system and balance your immune system. Enzymes will increase your digestive potential. Probiotics are also a vital part of your healing, as experts such as Donna Gates explain that up to 85% of your immunity is in your gut flora, which have often been wiped out by antibiotics and poor diet.

Two excellent resources for nutrition are *The Body Ecology Diet* by Donna Gates and *The Metabolic Typing Diet* by William Wolcott. Try to avoid foods that are toxic or stimulating, and foods that you are highly sensitive to. Tap away any cravings to these foods with EFT.

Consider exercise

Yes, this is a very contentious area for those overcoming ME.

Graded exercise has become almost a swear word in the ME communi-ty, as many have been misguided about appropriate exercise levels for their condition and have subsequently experienced more severe symp-toms as a result. However, be careful that you do not let this make you write off exercise altogether. In the early stages of the condition rest is vital, but as you rehabilitate, exercise can become equally important.

I had excellent advice from Peter Gladwell, a physiotherapist with expertise in ME at the Frenchay Hospital, in Bristol, UK. I started with 30 seconds per day on the treadmill, and built myself up by 1 minute per week until I reached 20 minutes. This took nearly 6 months. The key was to do it every day, and be gentle but consistent. Once I had built this up, I started floor exercising one repetition at a time, and add-ed one rep per week until I was up to 10 reps. Again, this took several months to achieve. Get some professional advice from someone who knows the condition, and listen to your own body to work out what is right for you. Above all, take it very slowly, and avoid pushing yourself at all costs.

Get your energy flowing

If you aren't ready to consider physical exercise, get your energy flowing with techniques such as tai chi, qi gong, or yoga. All these techniques have adaptations for those who are physically impaired (see the *Resources* section at the back of the book for details on related yoga books).

I have been to tai chi classes whilst overcoming ME, where the teacher has shown me the same exercises that able-bodied people were doing, but performed sitting in a chair. I have even met someone with ME who used to just go and lay on the floor at a tai chi class, and ben-efit from the relaxed atmosphere in the room while others practiced. Even just watching a tai chi DVD and deep breathing, or imagining yourself doing the exercises, can have a calming effect on your body, if you are unable to move.

If you would like a simple energy routine to get you started, then look at Donna Eden's 5-minute energy routine. This can be found in her book *Energy Medicine*, her *Energy Medicine Kit*, and also in the book *The Healing Power of EFT and Energy Psychology*, by David Feinstein, Donna Eden and Gary Craig. The routine can be adapted for physical impairment, and is an excellent way to get your energy flowing during long-term illness.

Find a Perrin practitioner

This will help to clear the congestion from your lymphatic system and will also provide you with a brilliant self-help technique to work on the congestion yourself. If you have not yet been diagnosed with ME, then you will also benefit from visiting a Perrin practitioner. This is because Raymond Perrin, who has worked with ME patients for almost two decades, has devised an osteopathic test for ME. He discovered that there are a number of physiological markers present in those with ME, which include a flattening of the thoracic spine; congestion in the lymphatics around the chest; a particularly sore point in the chest, which has been labeled Perrin's point; and a deadening of the cranial rhythm.

Find a PSYCH-K® practitioner

This extraordinary technique was created by Robert M. Williams. It will help you to reprogram your subconscious negative beliefs, and change them to positive ones, much like re-writing the software of a computer. In fact, I overcame the final hurdle of ME with a 45-minute PSYCH-K® session known as the "Core Belief Balance." This helped me shift destructive subconscious beliefs about the world as a dangerous place, and my expectation that things would always go wrong. With these beliefs shifted, the HPA axis switched off, as I was no longer perceiving danger and threat in my environment that was not there. Interestingly, I had been monitoring my heart rate on biofeedback software. On the day before I encountered this treatment, my resting heart rate was 106 beats per minute, and had been for some time. On the day after, it had returned to 72 beats per minute, which was presumably due to the overactive HPA axis returning to normal functioning. Preferably find an advanced PSYCH-K® practitioner or attend a training. Details of trainers can be found in the *Resources* section.

Educate yourself

Learn more about bodymind medicine. Read inspirational and positive material. Read about other people who have recovered. Read anything that makes your heart sing. There is a full list of recommended reading in the *Resources* section of this book.

Research, but don't search

Importantly, although educating yourself is vital, be certain that it does not become an obsession. A common phenomenon with ME is to be continually searching for answers to aid the healing process. It is very positive to take responsibility for your own healing. I truly believe that the lack of medical understanding about the condition is a gift on one level, as it means that more people with ME search inside themselves to aid their healing, rather than simply relying on a medic or a pill to heal their symptoms. On the downside, however, many people get lost in the search, continually looking outside themselves for answers from others instead of reflecting within and making simple, long-term changes. I have witnessed many people with the condition who have an almost obsessive quality about their searching (I know, as I was one of them!). Some of the tell-tale signs of this searching quality are:

• continuously trawling the Internet for answers in a non-structured way, often for hours at a time;

• reading a self-help book and then trying to make all the changes it suggests at once;

• having several self-help books on the go at once;

• undertaking three or four therapies at one time;

• becoming attached to other people's ideas about what is good for you rather than listening to your own body;

• attending every conference, lecture or workshop on ME, even if you have to travel a great distance and wear yourself out to do so;

• having a cupboard full of supplements, and purchasing and taking every supplement that has ever been recommended for use by those in recovery from ME (I've had clients who have been on 40+ supplements);

• abruptly changing your diet to match the advice of the latest nutritional book you have read, or following blanket nutritional advice without really listening to the needs of your body.

If we refer back to Gill Edwards' book, *Pure Bliss*, and her definition of "hard time" and "soft time," then we can see the effect that this constant searching is having on us. The trouble is that most of the time this searching is carried out in a hard-time cycle and thus is part of a tiring, pushing and pressured schedule to find, do, or achieve. A common thing that I have heard from clients who take this approach to recovery is "I'm doing all these things to get well, but deep down I know it's no use unless I do some work on myself", or "It's easy to focus on these things as it means I don't need to focus on myself."

In contrast, if we look for answers in a soft-time cycle it becomes research rather than searching. Research is educating yourself about the many approaches to healing from ME in a gentle and forgiving way. It is using your energy to gather resources, but only when you have the energy to do so, and stopping long before you tire. It is gently experimenting with suggestions and implementing them at a pace that suits you. It is considering whether advice is relevant to you before following it. If you research in this manner, you are much more likely to make progress, and discover what is right for you.

Stop watching the clock!

Although it is important to set small and achievable goals in your recovery from ME, it is vital that you do not set yourself a deadline for when you will be 100% well. I have witnessed many clients who have done this, and also originally did this myself to my own detriment. When I first went to see a naturopath about my condition, he estimated that it would take me 12 to 18 months to get well. My first response on leaving his office was "I bet I can do it in 6 months!"

Setting a deadline for health adds unnecessary pressure to the process of healing. Common examples are: "I need to be better by Christmas/my friend's wedding/next term/the new school year/the summer holidays/when I go traveling," etc. Setting a deadline of 100% health by a certain date serves only to exacerbate the situation and cause more stress, tension, and often disappointment.

The trouble is that if you set a deadline for healing, it is set by the same aspect of your personality that contributed to the illness in the first place – the "inner pusher." This is the part of yourself that sets unrealistic or pressured, self-conceived targets. It is great to set a goal to be 100% healthy, and this book is aimed at supporting you to achieve that goal on multiple levels; but for the best impact, try to ensure that this particular goal is not time-framed. Instead, time-frame the smaller steps to achieving the goal, which will depend on your level of recovery. These can include setting targets for the amount of rest and activity that you would like to take, the things you would like to incorporate from this book, or goals for healthy eating, for example.

Often the goal to achieve full health is motivated by financial concerns. It is important to realize that although financial concerns may represent a very real issue in your life, you cannot hurry your healing for financial reasons. The bodymind does not work in that way. It is important to resolve that nothing must come before your health. No amount of financial security can account for your health and well-being.

Avoid watching or reading things that depress you

While you are healing, stop watching and reading things that make you depressed or anxious such as the news, depressing documentaries about the suffering of others, and violent or depressing films. These will increase HPA axis stimulation and lower your immunity and your vibration. Remember to tap if you do see or hear something that disturbs you.

Take the "21-Day Complaint-Free Challenge"

Complaining will lower your energy and put you in a cycle of negativity. We have already established that thoughts create your world. According to motivational speaker Will Bowen, "When you eliminate complaining from your life you will enjoy happier relationships, better health and greater prosperity." He has created the "Complaint-Free" program which helps you redirect your mind towards a more positive and rewarding way of thinking. Visit http://www.acomplaintfreeworld. org to find out more.

Make a contribution to others

We are gregarious beings, and we thrive on social contribution. Do not let your illness disconnect you from contributing to those around you. Make someone a cup of tea, send someone an encouraging email, or write to someone who you know is feeling down. Making a contribution this way will help you to focus on the world outside your own healing.

Love yourself and others!

Self-love, and "loving thy neighbor," is a concept that has been bandied about for decades, and can often appear clichéd and over-emphasized. In reality, though, scientists in the field of bodymind medicine are suggesting that nothing could be more important.

Cell biologist Dr Bruce Lipton asserts that:

You can live a life of fear, or live a life of love. You have the choice! But I can tell you that if you choose to see a world full of love, your body will respond by growing in health. If you choose to believe that you live in a dark world full of fear, your body's health will be compromised as you physiologically close yourself down in a protective response.[89]

Immunologist Michael Ruff echoes these sentiments by saying that:

...to be healthy, well, and feel good our biology insists that we be in relationship to others, and through our connections, we are able to bring health to our bodymind.[90]

He also asserts that:

...love, compassion and relationship [....] are the human emotions that can heal us and lead to recovery from disease.[91]

EFT will help you clear your blocks to loving yourself and others, and return to a wholesome place within yourself, where you can give and receive love freely.

And finally...
Relax and discover the joy of living!

Consider the words of Esther and Jerry Hicks/Abraham in *Ask and it is Given*:

Your motion forward is inevitable; it must be. You cannot help but move forward. But you are not here on a quest to move forward; you are here to experience outrageous joy.

That is why you are here.[92]

Your aim is not just to heal, but to reconnect with the joy that is your birthright. So as you heal, remember (or discover) who you are. ME is your greatest teacher. If you allow yourself to learn your lessons from it, then a much richer life is available for you, not just in the future, but right now. A life where you no longer push or drive yourself; where you are present and happy; where you are free of your self-limiting beliefs and behaviors; where you are balanced and whole. With the tools outlined in this book, you can begin your new life today. You will need to do your own personal work in order to change, but know and understand that you are most definitely worth it. Welcome to the start of your new and brilliant life!

Conclusion

S o the new paradigm in biomedical sciences helps us understand that the mind and body are one. We have the scientific evidence of Dr Bruce Lipton, who shows us that that our beliefs create our biology by switching our gene expression on and off, and we can change these beliefs to benefit our health.

Thanks to the research of Dr Candace Pert, we also understand that our emotions are experienced through every cell in the body; and that to heal our emotional distress or physical disease, we have to heal the whole person.

And, thanks to Gary Craig, we have a highly versatile healing tool that can help us overcome emotional turmoil and physical illness easily and painlessly; a tool that we can use on ourselves any time we feel emotional or physical discomfort. I would like to leave you with two of Gary's favorite phrases. The first is that "We are on the first floor of a healing high-rise," meaning that the possibilities that EFT is opening for healing are just beginning. The second is "Try it on anything," and I encourage you to do so. In your hands you have a healing tool that you can use for any situation. Simple enough to use on yourself, yet so profound that it can positively affect your mind and body on every level.

I wish you peace, as your own journey with EFT unfolds.

Afterword

As I put the last finishing touches to this book it is still remarkable to me when I reflect how far I have come, by anyone's standards. A few years ago I could not properly dress myself, and I crawled around my house on all fours – an emotional and physical wreck. Today I am a picture of health, in fact healthier than I have ever been in my whole life. I practice yoga, I weight-train, I hill-walk, I cycle, and I have a zest for life like never before. I sing and dance, and my life is filled with joy. I am doing the work I love, and loving the work that I do. I have an abundance of amazing friends, and an incredible partner.

Of course all the opportunities that I have now were available to me before, but I did not realize my true potential. I lived in a different world where I was traumatized from childhood, and I had normalized obsessive-compulsive disorder, psychological imbalances, and numerous self-destructive and self-sabotaging behaviors. It is hard for me to relate to the memory of the old me, who was scared, insecure, paranoid, pained and a victim of my life experiences. The old me put on a very brave face as I went out into the world and achieved and functioned, but underneath I suffered. My ultimate consequence for wearing this mask was ME – my body broke down as I could no longer face the duality of my life. And what a gift it was, to bring me to this place where I finally know myself, and am congruent with how I feel and behave.

So as you consider what may seem a miraculous transformation, I invite you to understand and know this. All the tools that I used to transform are found in this book. And with the same tools, you have exactly the same opportunities available to you. In fact, it is my wish in writing this book that my story will not seem miraculous at all, but will be commonplace, as more and more people use these incredible tools to return to brilliant emotional and physical health. I look forward to hearing your own story of healing as you discover your true and amazing potential.

Sasha

June 2008

Appendix 1

EFT TAPPING POINTS

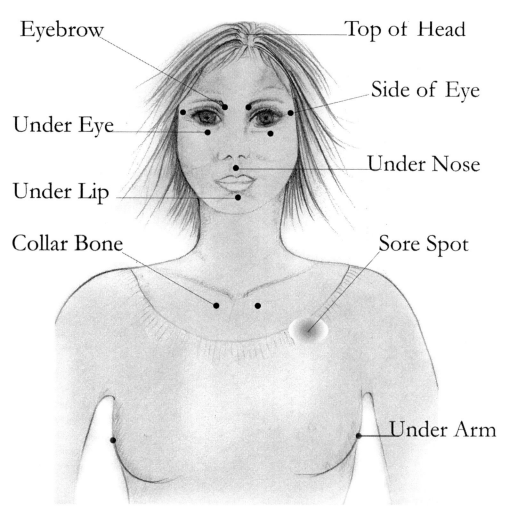

Eyebrow

Top of Head

Side of Eye

Under Eye

Under Nose

Under Lip

Collar Bone

Sore Spot

Under Arm

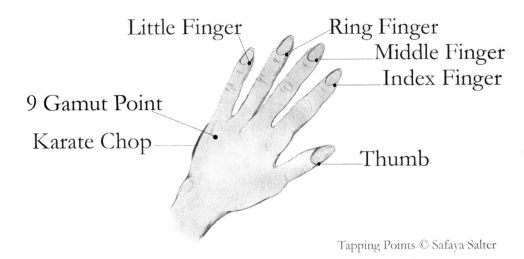

Tapping Points © Safaya Salter

Bibliography

Books

Bager, Jodi, and Jenny Lass. 2005. *Grain-Free Gourmet: Delicious Recipes for Healthy Living.* Vancouver: Whitecap Books.

Bloom, William. 2004. *SOULution: The Holisitic Manifesto.* London: Hayhouse.

Chopra, Deepak. 1994. *Journey Into Healing.* London: Rider Books.

Church, Dawson. 2007. *The Genie in Your Genes: Epigenetic Medicine and the New Biology of Intention.* Santa Rosa, CA: Elite Books.

Dossey, Larry. 1993. *Healing Breakthroughs: How Your Attitudes and Beliefs Can Affect Your Health.* London: Piatkus, 1993

Dworkis, Sam. 1997. *Recovery Yoga: A Practical Guide for the Chronically Ill.* New York: Crown Publications.

Eaton, John. 2005. *ME, Chronic Fatigue Syndrome and Fibromylgia: The Reverse Therapy Approach.* Authors OnLine.

Eden, Donna. 2003. *Energy Medicine: How to Use Your Body's*

Energies for Optimum Health and Vitality. London: Piatkus.

Edwards, Gill. 1992. *Living Magically.* London: Piatkus.

Edwards, Gill. 2006. *Pure Bliss: The Art of Living in Soft Time.* London: Piatkus.

Edwards, Gill. 2006. *Wild Love.* London: Piatkus.

Edwards, Gill. 2007. *Life is a Gift: A Practical Guide to Making Your Dreams Come True.* London: Piatkus.

Feinstein, David, Donna Eden, and Gary Craig. 2006. *The Healing Power of EFT and Energy Psychology.* London: Piatkus.

Fife, Bruce. 2005. *Cooking with Coconut Flour: A Delicious Low-Carb, Gluten-Free Alternative to Wheat.* Colorado Springs: Piccadilly Books.

Gates, Donna. 2006. *The Body Ecology Diet*, 9th ed. Decatur, GA: B.E.D. Publications.

Hamilton, David. 2006. *It's The Thought That Counts: The Astounding Evidence for the Power of Mind of Matter.* London: Hayhouse Inc.

Hamilton, David. 2007. *Destiny Versus Free Will.* Lonon: Hayhouse.

Hartmann, Silvia. 2002. *The Advanced Patterns of EFT.* Eastbourne, UK: Dragon Rising.

Hay, Louise. 2004. *You Can Heal Your Life.* London: Hay House.

Hicks, Esther, and Jerry Hicks. 2005. *Ask and it is Given.* London: Hayhouse.

Katie, Byron. 2002. *Loving What Is.* London: Rider and Co.

Lipton, Bruce. 2005. *The Biology of Belief.* Santa Rosa, CA:

Mountain of Love.

McTaggart, Lynne. 2003. *The Field: The Quest for the Secret Force of the Universe.* London: Element.

Mercola, Joseph. 2005. *The No-Grain Diet.* London: Hodder & Stoughton Ltd.

Millman, Dan. 2000. *Living on Purpose: Straight Answers to Universal Questions.* Novato, CA: H. J. Kramer & New World Library.

Millman, Dan. 1995. *The Life You Were Born to Live: Finding Your Life Purpose.* Tiburon, CA: H. J. Kramer & New World Library.

Millman, Dan. 2000. *The Way of the Peaceful Warrior*, 20th anniversary ed. Tiburon, CA: H. J. Kramer & New World Library.

Millman, Dan. 2004. *Sacred Journey of the Peaceful Warrior*, revised ed. Tiburon, CA: H. J. Kramer & New World Library.

Millman, Dan. 2007. *Wisdom of the Peaceful Warrior: A Companion to the Book That Changes Lives.* Tiburon, CA: H. J. Kramer & New World Library.

Myhill, Sarah. 2007. *Diagnosing and Treating Chronic Fatigue Syndrome*, 24th ed. http://www.drmyhill.co.uk/cfs_book.pdf.

Perrin, Raymond. 2007. *The Perrin Technique: How to Beat Chronic Fatigue Syndrome/ME.* London: Hammersmith Press.

Pert, Candace. 1999. *Molecules of Emotion: Why You Feel the Way You Feel.* London: Pocket Books.

Pert, Candace. 2007. *Everything You Need to Know to Feel Good.* London: Hayhouse.

Puri, Basant K. 2004. *Chronic Fatigue Syndrome: A Natural Way to Treat ME.* London: Hammersmith Press.

Tolle, Eckhart. 1999. *The Power of Now: A Guide to Spiritual*

Enlightenment. Novato, CA: New World Library.

Williams, Robert M. 2004. *The Missing Peace in Your Life*. Crestone, CO: Myrddin Publications.

Other media

Byrne, Rhonda. 2007. *The Secret* [DVD]. TS Productions LLC.

Chasse, Betsy, Marc Vicente, and William Arntz, directors. 2005. *What the Bleep Do We Know?*[DVD]. Revolver Entertainment.

Craig, Gary. EFT DVDs: The *EFT Foundation, Intermediate, and Honors Library.* http://www.emofree.com/.

Eden, Donna. 2004. *Energy Medicine Kit*. Sounds True Inc.

Articles

American Academy of Sleep Medicine. 2007. Chronic fatigue syndrome impairs a person's slow wave activity during sleep. May 7, http://www.sciencedaily.com/releases/2007/05/070501075253.htm.

BBc News. 2005, May 28. Scientists 'unlock ME genetics.'

http://news.bbc.co.uk/1/hi/health/4580051.stm

BBC News. 2008, May 5. Seven genetic types of ME found. http://news.bbc.co.uk/1/hi/health/7378440.stm.

Chia J.K., and A.Y. Chia. 2008. Chronic fatigue syndrome is associated with chronic enterovirus infection of the stomach. *Journal of Clinical Pathology* 61: 1–2.

Craig, Gary. Guidelines for using EFT on serious diseases [tutorial]. http://www.emofree.com/tutorial/tutorpsixteen.htm.

Craig, Gary. The Palace of Possibilities. http://www2.emofree.com/palace/palaceof1.htm#1.

Craig, Gary. The Personal Peace Procedure [tutorial]. http://www.emofree.com/tutorial/tutormthirteen.htm.

Lipton, Bruce. 2006–2007. The wisdom of the cells: Parts 1, 2 and 3. http://www.brucelipton.com. Derived from *The Wisdom of Your Cells: How Your Beliefs Control Your Biology*, published by Sounds True as an audio listening course on eight CDs, http://www.soundstrue.com.

Lipton, Bruce. 2006–2007. A romp through the quantum field. http://www.brucelipton.com.

Resources

Essential reading and viewing

There are a great deal of books and resources that I could recommend to further your understanding of the body–mind connection, and related topics. However, I am sensitive to the fact that if you have ME, your reading ability might be hampered by your current condition. Therefore, I have created a top 10. There is then a further reading and viewing list, if you should wish to expand your knowledge when your health improves.

All the resources below are available through my website **http://www.bodymindhealing.co.uk.**

Top 10 (in no particular order)

It's The Thought That Counts – **David Hamilton, Hayhouse, 2006**

This brilliant book explains bodymind science in a way that is highly accessible and easy to understand. An excellent introduction, with lots of examples of research and experimentation.

The Biology of Belief – Bruce Lipton, Mountain of Love, 2005

This is a fantastic explanation of how our thoughts affect our biology. It introduces us to epigenetics, explaining that it is not the genes that are in charge. Also available as a DVD or audiobook.

Everything You Need to Know to Feel Good – Candace Pert, Hayhouse, 2007

This outlines Candace Pert's research on the body as the subconscious mind.

The Healing Power of EFT and Energy Psychology – David Feinstein, Donna Eden and Gary Craig, Piatkus Books, 2006

A brilliant book outlining EFT and energy psychology – beautifully written, with practical instructions on how to use EFT.

The Secret – DVD, TS Productions LLC, 2007

A life-changing movie that will help you clearly understand the Law of Attraction.

Ask and it is Given – Esther and Jerry Hicks/Abraham, Hayhouse, 2005

A brilliant book on the Law of Attraction, with lots of practical exercises to help you manifest abundance in all areas of your life.

Pure Bliss: The Art of Living in Soft Time – **Gill Edwards, Piatkus, 2006**

This book will teach you how to live in "soft time," and help you return to a gentler way of living.

Loving What Is – **Byron Katie, Rider and Co., 2002**

A classic book that uses four questions to help you stop struggling against what is.

Healing Breakthroughs: How Your Attitudes and Beliefs Can Affect Your Health – **Larry Dossey, Piatkus, 1993**

A book by a medical doctor that is crammed full of examples of the mind working against the body. This book places great emphasis on the meaning behind the illness, and also illustrates how changing attitudes and beliefs can enhance the healing process.

The Energy Medicine Kit – **Donna Eden, Sounds True Inc., 2004**

This brilliant kit contains a DVD, audio CD and some cards for easy reference. It teaches you simple techniques for changing your energy levels and healing health conditions.

Science

Molecules of Emotion: Why You Feel the Way You Feel – **Candace Pert, Pocket Books, 1999**

An in-depth account of how Candace Pert discovered the link between our physical cell structures and our emotional experiences.

The Genie in Your Genes: Epigenetic Medicine and the New Biology of Intention – **Dawson Church, Elite Books, 2007**

A detailed, scientific exploration of the field of epigenetics.

What the Bleep do We Know? – **DVD, Revolver Entertainment, 2005**

An exploration of quantum physics, showing the convergence of science and spirituality. Also available as a book.

EFT

The EFT DVDs – **Gary Craig; visit http://www.emofree.com to order.**

This phenomenal DVD set by Gary Craig covers an enormous range of health issues and emotional problems. It includes nine sets of DVDs, ranging from the basics to using EFT for serious disease. These DVDs are world-renowned, and highly recommended if you want to learn more about EFT and see Gary Craig in action.

EFT for the Prevention and Treatment of Serious Diseases DVD Set – **Karl Dawson; visit http://www.efttrainingcourses.net to order.**

Highly recommended, particularly if you want to learn about Karl Dawson's Matrix Reimprinting work. Also a great explanation of the cycle of disease as outlined in this book.

Attracting Abundance with EFT – **Carol Look, AuthorHouse, 2005**

This classic and fabulous book contains 45 EFT exercises to help you overcome your blocks to attracting abundance.

Try in on Everything – **EFT DVD; visit http://www.tryitonevery-thing.com to order.**

This brilliant DVD features Jack Canfield, Joseph Mercola, Carol Look, Bruce Lipton, and many more. It is a great introduction to EFT.

Adventures in EFT – **Silvia Hartmann, Dragon Rising, 2000**

A great book on EFT for both practitioners and those working on themselves.

The Book of Reframes – **Stewart Robertson, Lulu, 2008**

This is an excellent resource for practitioners who want to help their clients reframe or change the meaning of situations, memories or events.

PSYCH-K®

The Missing Peace in Your Life – **Robert M. Williams, Myrddin Publications, 2004**

An introduction to the power of harnessing the subconscious mind.

Holistic health

Energy Medicine: How to Use Your Body's Energies for Optimum Health and Vitality – **Donna Eden, Piatkus, 2003**

A highly detailed manual with a multitude of exercises and activities for creating health and overcoming disease.

The Endorphin Effect: A Breakthrough Strategy for Holistic Health and Spiritual Wellbeing – **William Bloom, Piatkus, 2001**

Learn how to raise your own endorphin levels to manage pain and increase health and vitality.

Quantum Healing: Exploring the Frontiers of Mind/Body Medicine – **Deepak Chopra, Bantam Books Ltd, 1989**

An early classic from Deepak Chopra, who has always been at the leading edge of bodymind medicine.

Personal growth

You Can Heal Your Life [DVD] – **Louise Hay, Hay House Inc., 2008**

90-minute inspirational and entertaining movie charting the life and work of Louise Hay. If you get the extended version, there are also 4 hours of interviews with the likes of Cheryl Richardson, Candace Pert, and Greg Braden, alongside interactive affirmations.

Wild Love – **Gill Edwards, Piatkus, 2006**

A fabulous book for helping you find and connect with the true meaning of love. Helps you to love other people, yourself and life unconditionally!

Life is a Gift: A Practical Guide to Making Your Dreams Come True – Gill Edwards, Piatkus, 2007

A reminder that we are here for joy, and a guide to making your dreams come true.

The Astonishing Power of Emotions: Let Your Feelings Be Your Guide – Esther and Jerry Hicks, Hayhouse, 2007

An exploration of your emotional guidance system and how you can influence it to increase your positive emotions.

Be Your Own Life Coach: How to Take Control of Your Life and Achieve Your Wildest Dreams – Fiona Harrold, Mobius, New Edition, 2001

A guide to coaching your own life.

Take Time For Your Life: A Seven-step Program for Creating the Life You Want – Cheryl Richardson, Bantam, 2000

A seven-step program to help you get your life back in balance.

Spiritual development

The Way of the Peaceful Warrior – Dan Millman, H. J. Kramer, 2000 (20th Anniversary Edition)

This classic title, which is part fact and part fiction, uses a unique blend of Eastern philosophy and Western fitness to cultivate the true essence of a champion. It charts the journey of young gymnast Dan Millman, and his encounter with an unlikely spiritual teacher, Socrates, a garage attendant. This book contains timeless wisdom and is also available on DVD (although the DVD differs quite dramatically from the book, and both are recommended).

The Power of Now: A Guide to Spiritual Enlightenment – Ekhart Tolle, New World Library, 1999

A timeless classic helping you to develop present-moment awareness. Audio CDs are also available.

Nutrition

The Metabolic Typing Diet – William Walcott, Trish Fahey, Broadway Books, 2002 (New Edition)

Helps you to determine the right macro-nutrients for your body type, and implement them effectively.

The Body Ecology Diet – Donna Gates, Body Ecology, 2006 (9th Edition)

Helps you to rebuild your gut flora and immunity.

Grain-Free Gourmet: Delicious Recipes for Healthy Living – **Jodi Bager, Jenny Lass, Whitecap Books, 2005**

If you have grain intolerances, this book will show you how to make cookies, bread, pizza and muffins with almond flour. Also low GI foods, and minimal dairy. Recipes sweetened with honey.

Cooking with Coconut Flour: A Delicious Low-Carb, Gluten-Free Alternative to Wheat – **Bruce Fife, Piccadilly Books, 2005**

For an alternative to wheat, you can also make cookies, bread and muffins with coconut flour. Most recipes use coconut fat and milk as an alternative to dairy. Also sweetened with honey or stevia.

The No-Grain Diet – **Joseph Mercola, Hodder & Stoughton Ltd, New Edition 2005**

An excellent book if you cannot tolerate grains or high-carbohydrate foods.

Yoga

Beat Fatigue with Yoga – **Fiona Agombar, Thorsons, 1999**

A yoga program aimed at those with CFS/ME. Also available as a DVD.

Recovery Yoga: A Practical Guide for the Chronically Ill – **Sam Dworkis, Crown Publications, 1997**

Written by a yogi who at one point was severely debilitated with MS, this excellent book is suitable for healing from all health conditions.

There are exercises for those that are both disabled and able-bodied.

ME/CFS

The Perrin Technique: How to Beat Chronic Fatigue Syndrome/ME – Raymond Perrin, Hammersmith Press, 2007

A detailed explanation of the Perrin Technique, devised by osteopath Raymond Perrin, who has almost two decades' experience of working successfully with ME clients.

Chronic Fatigue Syndrome: A Natural Way to Treat ME – Basant K. Puri, Hammersmith Press, 2004

A detailed explanation of the need for correct supplementation of essential fatty acids in ME.

Recovery From CFS: 50 Personal Stories – compiled by Alex Barton; e-book available at http://www.alexbarton.co.uk/cfsrecovery-stories.htm

This excellent e-book is a goldmine of stories from people who have recovered form ME by a variety of different means. Compiled by UK life coach Alex Barton, who herself overcame ME, this is a great way of inspiring yourself by reading about other people's healing successes.

Websites

http://www.bodymindhealing.co.uk

Information about EFT, CFS/ME, plus links to all the products suggested in this book, including Holosync and Healing Rhythms software.

The Website also includes Sasha's Bodymind Training courses. Would you like to take a training course with Sasha? You can find Sasha's full schedule and book onto her courses, which include:

• EFT Practitioner Training – AAMET (Association for the Advancement of Meridian Energy Techniques) – Levels 1, 2 and 3;

• Joyful Recovery From CFS/ME – a 5-day course for those overcoming ME using the techniques outlined in this book.

• Discover Your Inner Tinkerbell! - It is Sasha's aim to help you not only heal, but to return to the joy of living that is your birthright. Join Sasha with her colleague, Jo Dance, in their 2-day workshop that helps you reconnect with the joy of living. This workshop incorporates EFT, NLP, drama, dance, and the Law of Attraction to help you find your inner joy. Also visit the site to share your positive experiences with others on the joy forum.

http://www.sashaallenby.com

Sasha's personal website with information about her books, articles, etcetera.

http://www.eft-me.co.uk

Website containing a collection of stories from those who have used EFT to overcome CFS/ME. It also contains case studies from practitioners.

If you have recovered from ME using EFT,

send your own healing story to:

sasha@bodymindhealing.co.uk

Other websites

EFT

http://www.emofree.com

Website of EFT founder, Gary Craig. Sign up for the newsletter, download the free EFT manual, buy the EFT DVDs, and get regular tips and advice on how to use EFT successfully.

http://www.emofree.com/Practitioners/referralMain.asp

Find an EFT practitioner.

http://www.uoom.com/aamet/main.php

Find an AAMET EFT practitioner.

http://www.efttrainingcourses.net

Website of EFT Master, Karl Dawson.

http://www.allergyantidotes.com

Website of Sandi Radomski, allergy expert.

http://www.eftworldmagazine.com

Website of *EFT World Magazine*, to which Sasha is a contributor.

PSYCH-K®

http://psych-k.com

Website of Robert M. Williams MA, creator of PSYCH-K®.

http://www.joyofliving.org.uk

Website of Mary Trenfield, UK PSYCH-K® trainer.

http://www.inneractiveconsulting.com

Website of Robin Graham, US PSYCH-K® trainer.

http://www.empoweredtransformations.com

Website of Dhebi DeWitz-Jensen, US PSYCH-K® trainer.

Science

http://www.brucelipton.com

Website of Dr Bruce Lipton.

http://www.drdavidhamilton.com

Website of Dr David Hamilton.

http://www.candacepert.com

Website of Dr Candace Pert.

Personal development

http://www.acomplaintfreeworld.org

Website of Will Bowen, of the *21-Day Complaint-Free Challenge*. Order your wrist-band, and take the challenge to help you become more positive.

http://www.thework.com

Website of Byron Katie, with lots of worksheets to implement "The Work."

Yoga

http://www.heartyoga.co.uk

An inspirational center for learning yoga or becoming a yoga teacher in the UK. The philosophy of the center is to "encourage people to let go of their rigidities, be they physical, emotional or conceptual, so that they can dance under the open sky." A brilliant place to learn yoga if you want to go beyond the Western approach, which has become very exercise-based, and learn with a flexible and open approach that supports your own personal development.

ME

http://www.theperrinclinic.com/

Website of Raymond Perrin and the Perrin Technique™.

Miscellaneous

www.uniquelyyou.vpweb.co.uk

Website of my highly esteemed business colleague, Jo Dance. Jo is a "Heal Your Life, Achieve Your Dreams" workshop leader, based on the work of Louise Hay, an NLP Master, Advanced EFT practitioner, and inspirational human being.

http://www.shirleykay.co.uk

Website of my naturopath and Perrin practitioner.

http://atouchlighter.co.uk

Website of Safaya Salter – illustrator of EFT tapping points, and EFT practitioner.

http://godfreydesigngroup.co.uk

Website of the company who designed the cover image for this book.

Acknowledgments

Thanks to my partner, Rupert Wood, who continues to be a guiding light in all that I do. Your wisdom and patience are astounding, and continue to fill me with light.

Thanks to all my family and friends who supported me in my recovery from ME. There are too many to mention you all individually, but you know who you are! Mum, Veronica, Sash, Rachel, Emma, Adam and Annie, you were all especially brilliant.

Thanks to EFT Master Karl Dawson. Your teachings accelerated my recovery, and this book wouldn't have happened without your inspiration.

Thanks to Gary Craig for being at the forefront of the new healing movement. You are an incredible, dynamic and unique human being.

Thanks to Mary Trenfield, Chris Walton, and Robin Graham for the PSYCH-K®.

Thanks to Fiona Harker and Jo Ventham for your excellent *Healthy ME* conferences, which were a breath of fresh air, for friendship (and for the laughter therapy!).

Thanks to my naturopath and Perrin practitioner, Shirley Kay, for the excellent role you played in my recovery. You kept me going in more challenging times and always believed in my ability to heal.

Thanks to my physiotherapist, Peter Gladwell, at the Frenchay Hospital, Bristol. Your sound and solid advice helped me to rehabilitate physically, and your professionalism, understanding, and time were so appreciated.

Thanks to Pete Yates and Anna Ingram at Heart Yoga for – in your words, Pete – "rattling my cage," and helping me to wake up!

Thanks to Jo Dance for being an inspirational and delightful business associate. You are a joy to work with.

Thanks to my editor, and dear friend, Alison Terry. It is such a pleasure working with you due to your passion for what you do. You are meticulous and brilliant!

Thanks to Becs, Susie, Lily and Russell for all your recent support.

Thanks to all at Strategic Book Publishing, especially Joanne, for all your advice on the book. You have made it so easy for me to get my work off the ground.

Thanks to Safaya Salter for the artwork. Also thanks to Sim at Godfrey Design Group, UK for the cover image.

Thanks to Louise Hay for the contribution you have made to the self-development movement, and also for creating Hay House – a goldmine of inspirational authors.

Acknowledgements

And finally thanks to all the authors, motivational speakers, and spiritual teachers who contributed to my healing: Bruce Lipton, David Hamilton, Candace Pert, Esther and Jerry Hicks, Dan Millman, Gill Edwards, Donna Eden, David Feinstein, Robert M. Williams, Eckhart Tolle, Neale Donald Walsch, Larry Dossey, Deepak Chopra, Byron Katie, Dawson Church, Greg Braden, Carol Look, Jack Canfield, Joseph Mercola, William Bloom, Lynne McTaggart, Raymond Perrin, and Bassant Puri. Long may you all continue to lead others into the light!

About The Author

S asha resides in the UK, in the South West of England. She lives in total joy after rediscovering herself through ME. She is often described as exuding pure love and joy, and has a special gift of being able to reach and connect with others. She is totally committed to helping her clients to return to the place of joy within themselves that she feels is their birthright.

Sasha has over 10 years' experience in holistic therapies and runs a busy private practice with national and international clients. She also has a busy workshop and training schedule.

Sasha has 15 years' experience of teaching, lecturing and facilitating in performing arts. She has worked using drama as a therapeutic tool with disaffected inner-city youths. She has had prominent positions with numerous Local Education Authorities, working as an adviser to senior management in schools on how to deal with problem behaviors. She has also taught drama in mainstream education, special education, and further education.

Sasha has a BA Hons Degree in Performing Arts from the University of Warwick, and a PGCE in Drama from the University of Central England. She also has the following holistic therapy qualifications: EFT Advanced Practitioner and Trainer (AAMET), Advanced PSYCH-K® Facilitator, Diploma in Life Coaching, Diploma in NLP, Diploma in Shiatsu, Teaching Certificate in Yoga, 1st and 2nd Degree Reiki, and OCR Level 2 in mat-based Pilates.

She has attended numerous continued professional development courses in ME/CFS.

Despite her vast range of qualifications, Sasha now focuses almost exclusively on EFT and PSYCH-K®. EFT is incredibly powerful at helping individuals to overcome their past, and PSYCH-K® can help to reprogram the subconscious mind with positive beliefs. These techniques ensure that personal change is fast, efficient, powerful and lasting.

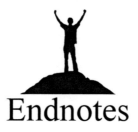

Endnotes

1. Sarah Myhill, D*iagnosing and Treating Chronic Fatigue Syndrome*.

2. Raymond Perrin, *The Perrin Technique: How to Beat Chronic Fatigue Syndrome/ME*.

3. Basant K. Puri, *Chronic Fatigue Syndrome: A Natural Way to Treat ME*.

4. American Academy of Sleep Medicine, Chronic fatigue syndrome impairs a person's slow wave activity during sleep.

5. J.K. Chia and A.Y. Chia, Chronic fatigue syndrome is associated with chronic enterovirus infection of the stomach.

6. BBC News, Scientists unlock 'ME genetics.'

7. BBC News, Seven genetic types of ME found.

8. Candace Pert, *Everything You Need to Know to Feel Good*, 35.

9. Larry Dossey, *Healing Breakthroughs: How Your Attitudes and Beliefs Can Affect Your Health*, 14.

10. Ibid., 76–77.

11. Ibid.

12. David Hamilton, *It's The Thought That Counts: The Astounding*

Evidence for the Power of Mind of Matter, 18–19.

13. Ibid., 19.

14. Ibid., 20.

15. Ibid., 20.

16. Ibid., 21.

17. Bruce Lipton, *The Biology of Belief*, 143.

18. Ibid., 137.

19. Ibid., 137–138.

20. Bruce Lipton, The wisdom of the cells, Part 1.

21. Bruce Lipton, *The Biology of Belief*, 48.

22. Ibid., 50, quoting Charles Darwin (Charles Darwin, *Life and Letters*. London: Murray).

23. Ibid., 50.

24. Ibid., 51.

25. Ibid.

26. Ibid.

27. Ibid.

28. Bruce Lipton, The wisdom of the cells, Part 2.

29. Ibid.

30. Ibid.

31. Ibid.

32. Bruce Lipton, *The Biology of Belief*, 135.

33. Bruce Lipton, A romp through the quantum field.

34. Bruce Lipton, *The Biology of Belief*, 166.

35. Ibid., 167–168.

36. Ibid., 166.

37. Bruce Lipton, The wisdom of the cells, Part 3.

38. Bruce Lipton, *The Biology of Belief*, 127.

39. Bruce Lipton, The wisdom of the cells, Part 1.

40. Bruce Lipton, *The Biology of Belief*, 172.

41. Ibid., 149.

42. Ibid., 150.

43. Ibid., 152.

44. Ibid., 152.

45. Dr Bruce Lipton, quoted on http://www.emofree.com.

46. Candace Pert, *Everything You Need to Know to Feel Good*, 29–32.

47. Ibid., 29.

48. Ibid., 30.

49. Ibid.

50. Ibid.

51. Ibid.

52. Ibid., 31.

53. Ibid.

54. Ibid., 32.

55. Ibid., 171.

56. Ibid.

57. Ibid.

58. Ibid., 172.

59. Candace Pert, quoted on http://www.emofree.com.

60. Candace Pert, *Everything You Need to Know to Feel Good*, 11.

61. Ibid., 47.

62. Ibid., 48.

63. Ibid.

64. Ibid.

65. Ibid.

66. Ibid., 232.

67. Ibid.

68. Ibid., 80.

69. Candace Pert, *Molecules of Emotion: Why You Feel the Way You Feel*, 305.

70. Bruce Lipton, *The Biology of Belief*, 113.

71. Candace Pert, *Everything You Need to Know to Feel Good*, 70.

72. Ibid.

73. David Feinstein, Donna Eden, and Gary Craig, *The Healing Power of EFT and Energy Psychology*, 29.

74. Ibid., 35.

75. Gary Craig, The Personal Peace Procedure [tutorial].

76. Gary Craig, Guidelines for using EFT on serious diseases [tutorial].

77. Ibid.

78. Ibid.

79. http://www2.emofree.com/palace/palaceof1.htm#1

80. Sandi Radomski, http://www.allergyantidotes.com.

81. EFT DVDs Specialty Series 2, available from http://www.emofree. com.

82. Candace Pert, *Everything You Need to Know to Feel Good*, 87.

83. Gill Edwards, *Pure Bliss: The Art of Living in Soft Time*, 15.

84. Esther and Jerry Hick, *Ask and it is Given*, 114.

85. Candace Pert, *Molecules of Emotion: Why You Feel the Way You Feel*, 277.

86. Ibid., 295.

87. Sam Dworkis, *Recovery Yoga: A Practical Guide for the Chronically Ill,* 33.

88. Candace Pert, *Everything You Need to Know to Feel Good*, 111.

89. Bruce Lipton, *The Biology of Belief,* 144.

90. Candace Pert, *Everything You Need to Know to Feel Good*, 173.

91. Ibid., 174.

92. Esther and Jerry Hicks, *Ask and it is Given*, 114.

Printed in the United Kingdom by
Lightning Source UK Ltd., Milton Keynes
140617UK00001BH/1/P